Vintage Dirt Bikes
Enthusiast's Guide

Doug Mitchel

Published by:
Wolfgang Publications Inc.
P.O. Box 223
Stillwater, MN 55082
www.wolfpub.com

Legals

First published in 2014 by Wolfgang Publications Inc.,
P.O. Box 223, Stillwater MN 55082

© Doug Mitchel, 2014

All rights reserved. With the exception of quoting brief passages for the purposes of review no part of this publication may be reproduced without prior written permission from the publisher.

The information in this book is true and complete to the best of our knowledge. All recommendations are made without any guarantee on the part of the author or publisher, who also disclaim any liability incurred in connection with the use of this data or specific details.

We recognize that some words, model names and designations, for example, mentioned herein are the property of the trademark holder. We use them for identification purposes only. This is not an official publication.

ISBN 13: 978-1-929133-31-4

Printed and bound in U.S.A.

Vintage Dirt Bikes Enthusiast's Guide

1971 BSA Victor	Page 6
1966 Bultaco Matador	Page 9
1977 Bultaco Model 191 Sherpa T	Page 12
1971 Bultaco Pursang MK IV	Page 15
1975 Can-Am 175 TNT	Page 18
1982 Can-Am Sonic 500	Page 21
1976 CZ Falta 400 Replica	Page 24
1970 Ducati 350 Scrambler	Page 26
1977 Harley-Davidson MX250	Page 29
1973 Harley-Davidson SR 100	Page 32
1977 Hodaka 250 Thunderdog	Page 35
1971 Hodaka Ace B Model	Page 37
1974 Hodaka Super Rat	Page 40
1962 Honda CL72	Page 43
1974 Honda CR125 Elsinore	Page 45
1972 Honda XL250 Motosport	Page 48
1970 Kawasaki F21M	Page 51
1974 Kawasaki F7	Page 54
1974 Kawasaki F9-B	Page 56
1974 Kawasaki KX250	Page 58
1978 Kawasaki KX250	Page 60
1974 Kawasaki KX450	Page 63
1969 Maico 360 X-4A	Page 65
1973 Monark GS125	Page 68
1974 Montesa Cota 123T	Page 71
1975 Montesa Cota 172	Page 74
1975 Montesa Cota 25	Page 76
1972 OSSA 250 Mick Andrews Replica	Page 78
1976 OSSA Desert Phantom 250	Page 81
1972 OSSA 250 Pioneer	Page 83
1973 OSSA Six-Day Replica	Page 86
1970 OSSA Hybrid	Page 89
1970 Penton Berkshire 100	Page 91
1971 Penton Berkshire 100 Vintage comp.	Page 93
1975 Penton Jack Pine 175	Page 95
1973 Penton Jack Pine 175	Page 98
1971 Penton Six-day 125	Page 101
Interview with John Young	Page 104
1973 Penton Wassell Trials 125	Page 106
1974 Rickman w F21 Engine	Page 19
1976 Rokon RT340 Automatic	Page 112
1967 Triumph T100C Tiger	Page 115
1967 Triumph Tiger Cub	Page 118
1966 Triumph T120C TT	Page 120
1973 Triumph TR5T	Page 123
1968 Yamaha DT 1	Page 125
1971 Yamaha RTB1 - 360	Page 127
1967 Yamaha YM2C Big Bear Scrambler	Page 129
1974 Yankee 500Z	Page 133
1967 Zundapp 100cc ISDT	Page 136
1973 Zundapp GS125	Page 139
Wolfgang Books	Page 142

Dedication

To all of those who rode in the past, continue to ride today and hope to ride in the future, thank you for letting me share in your experiences.

Acknowledgements

Creating the materials needed to fill the pages of a new book is rewarding and challenging. I lean on those in the sport for information and leads and in the case of this effort I need to give one man a huge pat on the back. He contacted me after learning of my needs and then set me up with 99% of the collectors in this book. Were it not for **Tony Glueck** and his terrific band of off-road brothers I would still be stuck on a berm with no hopes of finishing the heat race. Once he told me of who to contact and what their collection held, I reached out and found them to be agreeable to my efforts and opened the doors to their homes and collections. I owe Tony a huge debt of gratitude. Not only did he put me in touch with all the required people and machines, his own knowledge and experience in the sport is something of legend. His own collection of two-wheeled vehicles is also vastly entertaining.

I also extend my wishes of thanks to the others listed here. If it weren't for their passion for the sport and knowledge of their gear the world would be a sadder place to live. To the following I tip my helmet, in no particular order:

Rex Cusumano
Gary Lingbeck
Norm Carroll
Rod Gorzny
John Young

Dennis Jones
Mike Reusch
David Freeman
Roger Smith

Clay Setzer
Scott Wallenberg
Keith Campbell
Brad Powell

Geoff Mellinger
Buzz Walneck
Tom Reese
Richard Backus

Introduction

I am fairly well-versed in the world of motorcycles as long as they are destined for street use. Being born and raised in the suburbs of Chicago there was no location that was designed for the use of off-road machines and that kept my focus on those that traveled the tarmac. As I delved into this new world I was amazed at the amount of collectors who had terrific arrays of machines plus years of experience riding off-road. A few have even participated as sanctioned competition factory racers during the birth of the sport in the USA.

As I approached each collector I learned more about the sport. Not only did these guys gather an amazing collection of machines they had stories and history for each and every one. A wealth of technical data was shared with only a few exceptions. In these cases it wasn't something they didn't know of, it was simply a lack of printed evidence in the form of ads, factory brochures or magazine stories. Gathering that aspect of the book was the most challenging for me. The cycles weren't hard to find but some of the information needed has yet to appear.

A couple of people I knew from the street side of the sport had machines that fit the profile but the vast majority was brand new faces and names. After spending time with them and being allowed to capture the images seen here I feel as if I made new friends as well. I hope that they realize how important it is to me and a project of this nature to allow me to take so much of their time to complete the work.

As a side note, doing the **Motorcycle Ratings** for each model is always a beast. The owners all had places they liked to use and visit to get parts, and I did some of my own searching online to locate the same. Some machines featured here can just about be built from scratch while others are a bit more obscure. It makes sense that if only 100 or so of a certain model was made, an abundance of parts is not something that exists. When I speak of the **Final Value vs Restoration Costs,** part of that factor is based on the rarity of the machine itself. If it is one of only 100 made and has been lovingly restored the value is going to be higher regardless of how easy parts are to find and how easy it went together. The value of anything is based partly on how much another person is willing to pay and that is one of the more nebulous figures in the universe, so please keep that in mind. Also, the **Ease of Restoration** is partly based on how easy it is to locate the needed bits. If you can buy every nut, bolt, fender and piston at the corner store that factor would be 7 out of 7, but sadly that level of convenience never comes into play.

Overall I hope you enjoy the array of makes and models featured here. Before anything began we conferred with 6 or 7 experts in the field and gathered their "must haves" for the book. A vast majority of them were located without too much trouble but as always a few remain elusive. I'm sure they are out there, but logistics and time are not always on my side. I welcome comments and input so as to create even better projects in the future.

Ride safe and have a great time!

1971 BSA Victor 250

If not for the four-stroke engine, the 1971 Victor would be on the same playing field as the remaining 99% of the market.

Owner: Rex Cusumano

BSA began its journey in 1906 as a maker of firearms. The BSA moniker stands for British Small Arms, or at least did until their motorcycle production began in the early '20s. In between those two events the company started producing engines that were used in other motorcycles. When the 1920s got rolling a few complete cycles bearing the BSA logo were produced and the company went on to become one of cycling's storied marques.

Not wanting to miss out on the off-road craze of the late '60s and early '70s, BSA also threw their hat in the ring. The formula of the period seemed to be to produce one version of your off-road models for on and off road riding with the alternate designed for pure off-road action. The 1971 BSA sales brochure shows us four different variations of their off-road machines. A trio of 500cc models was teamed with a pair of 250cc variants that seemed to be more rider friendly to new riders. The Victor 500-Trail was complete with lights and a heat shield on the exhaust that was intended for on and off road use. The Victor 500-MX was for racing and nothing else, proven by the lack of lighting and stripped down features along with added power. The Gold Star

500-SS was the street scrambler edition.

The 250cc models were more similar to each other without either one being a rugged down and dirty race machine. The Gold Star 250-SS was the street scrambler with a close-fitting front fender and a dry weight of 290 pounds. The Victor 250-Trail featured the high-mounted front fender, taller handlebars with the cross brace and a weight that was 3 pounds lighter than the Gold Star. An aluminum tank on the Victor also helped to save a few ounces over the Gold Star.

Both versions carried a single-cylinder engine that displaced 250cc, a four-cycle motor which was an oddity in the off-road arena. A 28mm Amal carb was used on both as was the four-speed gearbox. The rubber on the Victor was a bit more aggressive but still capable of street use. The Victor also claimed an extra ½ inch of ground clearance over the more subtle Gold Star. The remaining spec sheet comparisons showed the two smaller models sharing every facet of their construction. With the exception of the bigger displacement and added power of the 500cc models all five machines shared most of their dimensions. The Victor 500-MX cost a buyer $1183 in 1971 and I can't imagine that the 250's were a lot cheaper based on their similarity to their larger siblings.

As we have learned time and time again, by the time 1971 came around the Japanese were continuing to make inroads into the cycle market both here and abroad. The BSA brand had suffered earlier setbacks as had most of the British marques, but the growing off-road market didn't seem to have room for another batch of machines that weren't superior to the competition. Although well-built and nicely designed the BSA effort fell short on the berms of the buying public and was soon lost in the dust.

The 250cc single and 4-speed transmission are a unit design - both contained in one case, which made for a nice compact package.

With the exception of the Victor 500-MX model, every other BSA off-road cycle for 1971 wore this decorative heat shield.

A solitary gauge - the speedo - was mounted to the handlebars.

1971 BSA Victor 250 Trail Model Highlights

The four-stroke engine used in the Victor was unusual for the type of machine being offered but was somewhat easier to ride.

The appearance of the Victor 250 was vastly appealing with the silver painted frame and chrome tank accented by black sections of paint.

The dimensions of the Victor 250 Trail and its sibling were nearly identical with only a few minor adjustments between the two.

The taller handlebars complete with cross-brace told you the Victor 250 Trail was the more serious off-road model.

The front fender riding high above the tire was another indication of the Trail's intent.

Slightly knobbier tires at both ends were yet another clue to the Victor 250 Trail's expected actions.

Priced on par with most of the European machines gave the BSA range some protection for the incoming Japanese competition.

Uncluttered lines and a great graphics package added a lot of appeal to the BSA Victor, but that was not enough to sustain the model or the brand.

Aluminum was used to craft the tank on the Victor 250-Trail model and its capacity was the same 2.5 gallons found on the Gold Star 250-SS.

Motorcycle Specifications:
1971 BSA Victor 250-Trail
Wheelbase: 54 inches
Weight: 287 Pounds (dry)
Seat Height: 32 inches
Displacement: 250cc
Fuel Delivery: 28mm Amal Concentric Carburetor
Fuel Capacity: 2.5 Gallons
Horsepower: 22.5@8250 RPM
Top Speed: N/A   **MSRP:** N/A

Motorcycle Ratings:
Available Examples: 2 out of 7
Availability of Replacement Parts: 2 out of 7
Ease of Restoration: 2 out of 7
Final Value vs Restoration Costs: 2 out of 7

1966 Bultaco Matador

The right side of the Matador shows off the chrome fenders, case covers and a portion of the adjustable exhaust system.

Owner: John Young

Bultaco was born in 1958 and named after Francesco "Paco" Bultó. Long time engineer and director of the racing program for Montesa, Paco left to form is own company when Montesa made plans to pull the plug on factory racing. With Paco came a number of key Montesa employees and by 1959 they were able to bring to market the first of their new machines.

Fast forward to 1965 when the Matador MK II takes to the streets and trails. It was designed for use on the street and trails in a number of configurations. By utilizing one of Bultaco's unique features, the Bultaco easily-modified exhaust system, the rider could adapt his Matador to take on almost any terrain and condition. The perky single-cylinder, two-stroke engine displaced 244cc and developed 22 horsepower at 6500 RPM, not a bad feat for a machine weighing only 250 pounds before adding fuel. Reviews in CYCLE and CYCLE WORLD in 1969 raved of the natural ability the Matador seemed to possess and how easily it handled changing surfaces and terrain. To add to its list of glories, the Matador was nicely finished with chrome fenders and more chrome on the engine case covers. The two-tone paint lent an air of formality to the spunky performer,

Displacing 244cc and fed by a single 24mm carb the Matador delivered a very useful power range to suit almost any riding situation.

The chrome engine case covers look a bit out of place on an off-road machine but the Matador was equipped for street riding too.

The exhaust on the Matador was designed for easy changes to better suit different riding situations.

and only $895 was required for this do-it-all performer.

The Matador went through several levels of revision until the end in 1979. The MK II ran from 1967-1969. The MK III was sold from 1967-1970 the featured bike here being a MK III. The MK IV had a short life of two years between 1971 and 1972 with the next change, MK V and MK IX from '75 to '78. The final iteration was the MK X which was available from 1977 until the doors closed on Bultaco in 1979. The MK IX and X were powered by an upscale 350cc two-stroke while the rest used the smaller motor.

The MK III seen here, as well as all the rest, are fed by a 24mm Amal carburetor from Spain. The 244cc engine could get the Matador to a top speed of 72 MPH after rowing through all five gears.

Bultaco's innovative exhaust system could be tuned by the rider to alter not only

> **Motorcycle Specifications:**
> **1966 Bultaco Matador**
> **Wheelbase:** 53.5 inches
> **Weight:** 250 Pounds (1/2 tank of fuel)
> **Seat Height:** 30.75 inches
> **Displacement:** 244cc
> **Gearbox:** 5-Speed
> **Final Drive:** Chain
> **Fuel Delivery:** 24mm Amal
>   (Spanish) Carburetor
> **Fuel Capacity:** 3.5 Gallons
> **Horsepower:** 20@6500 RPM
> **Top Speed:** 72 MPH
> **MSRP:** $840
> **Production:** 1959-1979 (all versions)
>
> **Motorcycle Ratings:**
> **Available Example:** 1 out of 7
> **Replacement Parts Availability:**
>   4 out of 7
> **Ease of Restoration:** 3 out of 7
> **Final Value vs Restoration Costs:**
>   3 out of 7

the amount of power produced, but where in the RPM band that power came on.

An online check for machines and parts revealed a whole bunch of available parts but not a single machine to work on. No way to tell how many Bultacos were built in their short 20 year run, but it appears as if all they sold are still being held under wraps. The Matador had a nearly 15 year production run when totaling every version made, which for a single model isn't too shabby.

Bultaco Matador Model Highlights

Perky handling and an adaptable exhaust gave riders of all sizes a chance to enjoy the traits of the Matador.

Good power and a decent weight delivered riders on a healthy jaunt upon their requests.

The fuel tank held 3-1/2 gallons of fuel which provided hours of entertainment .

Brightly chromed fenders and engine case covers add a bit of sizzle.

The MSRP of $840 was on par with other machines of the day, but the Matador's flexibility and features made it seem like a better value than most.

20 horsepower was available at 6500 RPM, strong output for the day.

The simple layout, compact size, and good power made and the Matador a popular bike when new.

Capable of holding up to 3.5 gallons of fuel the Matador had a better than average range.

Designed for light weight, the minimalist heat shield provided minimal protection as well.

1977 Bultaco Model 191 Sherpa T 350

Although a petite machine the overall packaging of the Sherpa T 350 is rather stout in appearance.

Owner: Rex Cusumano

In a fairly short amount of time the Bultaco brand earned a reputation for building a wide variety of motorcycles for off-road use. They had models for MX, trials, enduros and even a few for street use too. One of the more recognized names was the Sherpa named after the extremely talented mountaineers from Nepal.

The Sherpa was sold in smaller displacements in the early days, but later grew into either a 250cc or 3500cc model. The first 250cc came in 1970 and the 350 followed in 1972. Any die-hard Bultaco fan will present the machines by model number, not by name. The 1977 edition shown here is Model 191 and was a 199 for the '78 version. The Sherpa T was designated for use in trials competition and was built to capitalize on the unique features found on almost every trials cycle.

A trials rider likes a machine that's light and narrow with plenty of ground clearance. With 10.2 inches of clarance and a seat height of 32.5 inches, the 191 came with all the right features - though the seat is barely used in a trials competition due to the stand-up riding styles used by most riders.

Model 191 weighed only 203.9 pounds before fuel. The tank held only 1.2 gallons, so even when full it wasn't a big setback in terms of added pounds.

The Bultaco logo always included the gloved hand giving a thumbs-up along with the Cemoto name.

In keeping with the narrow theme, the exhaust turns up, around and down - always tucked in close to the engine and frame.

The small boxlike feature is actually the muffler and did a decent job of keeping things quiet.

Power came via the single-cylinder, 326cc two-stroke engine that was fitted with a 25mm Amal carb and mated to a five-speed transmission. 21 horsepower was on tap at 5000 RPM which was well suited for trials riding. With the small capacity of the fuel tank it's obvious that the physical size will be on par with a 1.2 gallon capacity. The tank and minimal body work is mounted to a steel tube frame finished in silver. Betor suspension is found at both ends, a brand that was well known for doing a good job in the trials arena. The 52.3 inch wheelbase also added to the precise handling of the Model 191, Sherpa T. Helping to keep things narrow the exhaust snakes its way under the fuel tank and exits at a rectangular muffler mounted directly to the side rails of the chassis. Drum brakes are located at each hub and the slow pace of a trials event would never overtax them. No lighting or extra conveniences are found the Model 191 in an effort to save every ounce possible.

Motorcycle Specifications:
1977 Bultaco Model 191
Wheelbase: 52.3 inches
Weight: 203.9 Pounds (dry)
Seat Height: 32.5 inches
Displacement: 326cc
Gearbox: 5-Speed
Final Drive: Chain
Fuel Delivery: 25mm Amal Carburetor
Fuel Capacity: 1.2 Gallons
Horsepower: 21@5000 RPM
Top Speed: N/A
MSRP: $1195

Motorcycle Ratings:
Available Examples: 2 out of 7
Replacement Parts Availability:
  5 out of 7
Ease of Restoration: 3 out of 7
Final Value vs Restoration Costs:
  3 out of 7

Finding complete examples of a Sherpa T isn't impossible and the availability of parts is amazing. Nearly every nut and bolt used to build them new can be found with a few clicks of your mouse. Those who have spent time on the saddle tell of how pleasant the Sherpa T was to ride, which tells me it's great place to begin.

Bultaco Model 191 Sherpa T 350 Model Highlights

Those who got an opportunity to ride a Sherpa T were largely pleased with the ease of control the small machine offered.

Stylish graphics on the body work helped draw buyers into the showrooms and the $1195 price tag didn't frighten them away.

Plenty of ground clearance allowed the Model 191 to be ridden over some heavy terrain with ease.

The 326cc engine produced 21 horsepower at 5000 RPM, riders had a selection of five gears to suit changing track conditions

The relatively compact wheelbase of only 52.3 inches was a part of the reason the Model 191 rode as well as it did.

The compact design of the Model 191 is evident from any angle and the exhaust path can be seen in greater detail too.

The nature of the beast in trials events was to keep things narrow and the tiny 1.2 gallon tank on the Model 191 was all of that.

A 326cc, two-cycle single-cylinder engine is on hand to power the Sherpa T 350 into places other cycles in its class might not go.

1971 Bultaco Pursang MK IV Model 68

The two-tone paint helps to set the Pursang aside as a machine that includes style and performance in a tidy package.

Owner: Rex Cusumano

After being created in 1958, the Bultaco brand became a strong player in the off-road arena. Their founder had previously been with Montesa and brought plenty of knowledge with him to the new marque.

Of the many models that were offered through the Bultaco dealerships, the Pursang was first seen in 1965 and rose quickly to the top of the ranks. Considered to be one the best looking and performing machines in that genre, the Pursang carried a variety of traits to earn the glory it received. Several versions of the Pursang were sold during its run and engine displacements ran the gamut from 125cc up to 370cc. The MK IV carried a 244cc version of the two-stroke powerplant in its frame and proved to be one of the more potent combinations of power and handling. The MK IV was sold for two years, 1971 and 1972 and riders really took advantage of what the Pursang had to offer.

A dry weight of 220 pounds was within range of others in the field but the longer wheelbase and outstanding torque of the engine put it ahead of the class. The power was available at nearly every RPM and even novice riders gained an advantage when aboard a Pursang. The name Pursang, or pur-sang, can be loosely translated into "thoroughbred" and when pitted against rivals at any off-road event the other riders knew why it had been given that name.

The market for off-road machines was flooded with 250cc selections and the Pursang's combination of weight, power, handling and style kept it at the top of its class from its inception. The success the Pursang claimed turned it into one of the best-selling models when new, and keeps it at the top of most collectors shopping lists today.

Specifications for Model 68 were impressive and added up to the winning machine it was designed to be. Almost 10 inches of ground clearance motivated by 35 horsepower sent through a five-speed gearbox may not have appeared to be anything outstanding, but one ride at your local track told you otherwise. For a machine with that much ground clearance the saddle height was only 31 inches making it accessible to even riders shorter in stature. Sold in two variations, the Pursang provided buyers with options to best suit their own needs. The scrambler version rolled on a 19 inch wheel up front fitted with a universal tire, while the motocross option used a 21 inch front wheel with knobby tires at both ends.

The proportions of the bodywork remain classic today including the shape of the 1.2 gallon fuel tank. The saddle was comfortable and offered more than enough padding for a day at the track. Being a true race machine the Pursang did not provide a passenger with any foot pegs or grab straps. The complete lack of lighting was another sign of its true purpose, which was winning at race tracks around the country and abroad.

All of these factors played a role in giving the Pursang its desired status with collectors and riders then as well as now. Not only is it a truly great machine to ride, available examples are more common than many others and finding parts is nowhere near as challenging as others in this book.

The 244cc engine of the Pursang delivered ample horsepower and torque to make the MK IV a high performance machine.

With a capacity of only 1.18 gallons, the tank on the Pursang retained a graceful shape that really boosted the overall appearance.

The gentle contours of the tail section only added to the terrific design of the Pursang.

When the motocross version was chosen you got a machine that was potent and attractive making it a sought after collectible today.

The fuel cap wears the "thumbs-up" logo that the company employed since its inception in 1959.

While locating one as pristine as the bike seen here would be like winning the lottery, parts to bring one back to life looks like a viable option when viewing common online sources.

Bultaco Pursang MK IV Model Highlights

The 244cc, single-cylinder, two-stroke engine in the Pursang was a potent performer that moved the 220 pound machine with ease.

Nearly 10 inches of ground clearance allowed the Pursang to travel over the most rugged terrain you could find.

A saddle height of only 31 inches made the Pursang user-friendly to smaller riders.

Sold in two versions, the motocross option sold the most and gave riders a distinct advantage over their rivals.

The engine produced a very wide torque range that delivered power at almost any RPM.

Styling was considered to be the best and helped push the Pursang to the top of many collector's most-wanted list.

The saddle was a comfortable perch for days at the track and having no lights the Pursang was not equipped for street use.

The Pursang was available as a scrambler model that came with less aggressive tires and a smaller 19 inch wheel up front.

Availability of parts today makes the Pursang one of the easier models to use and continue riding.

Motorcycle Specifications:
1971-1972 Bultaco Pursang MK IV Model 68
Wheelbase: 55.9 inches
Weight: 220.4 Pounds (dry)
Seat Height: 31-3/32 inches
Displacement: 244cc
Gearbox: 5-Speed
Final Drive: Chain
Fuel Delivery: 32mm Amal Carburetor
Fuel Capacity: 1.18 Gallons
Horsepower: 35.2@8000 RPM
Top Speed: N/A   **MSRP:** N/A
Production: 1971-1972
Motorcycle Ratings:
Available Examples: 2 out of 7
Replacement Part Availability: 4 out of 7
Ease of Restoration: 4 out of 7
Final Value vs Restoration Cost: 3 out of 7

1975 Can-Am T'NT 175

Rex Cusumano

The Can-Am brand came to be in 1973 as a result of a select group of people who sought more than the current rash of off-road machines could offer. The results of their efforts were seen as four different models designed to suit the demands of riders who asked for more. Of the four, the 175 T'NT (Track and Trail) appealed to most riders. The 175 MX-1 was its sibling and while still delivering a great package of features it was built more for the racing rider.

The 175 T'NT was powered by an engine that was acquired through Rotax. Bombardier was the parent of the Can-Am brand and Rotax was also one of their subsidiaries. Still built in the two-stroke fashion the Rotax engine used a rotary valve arrangement for more power and a broader power band. A single cylinder engine was a common denominator in the off-road arena and the T'NT's unit displaces 173.6cc. There was a 125 T'NT model too but the 175 is our feature today. Most of the specs on the 175 were not unusual or terribly unique but the quality of the components was higher than many found at other dealers in the day. The fenders were still a plastic-like material, but Can-Am used a material that was highly resistant to cracking and breaking in contrast to the units found on nearly every other model sold.

The high-mounted exhaust was seen on the left side of the 175 T'NT and did a great job of keepings quiet.

The vivid graphics placed on an off-white fuel tank was a great choice for visibility and the cross-bar on the handle bars was a common feature for off-road machines.

Before adding fuel the 175 T'NT weighed only 222 pounds and the engine produced 25 horsepower which was a great pairing of weight and power. Ground clearance sat at 9 inches but the seat height was a more useable 30 inches, a number that was suited to far more riders than some of machines with heights of 33 inches.

Prior to releasing the new machines to the retail crowd, Bombardier decided that 40% of the new machine could be out sourced as long as the products selected were of the highest caliber. Front forks from Betor, rear shocks by Girling and the CDI ignition from Bosch were among the vendors selected. The 175 T'NT was designed for use as an enduro machine, thus a few components lent themselves to street use. The speedometer, turn signals and head and tail lights were all indications of this path while the MX-1 wore none of those items due to its true race nature.

As it often happens in the corporate world, numbers speak volumes and the brand was licensed away in 1983 and ceased production in 1987. The arrival of the Japanese contingent played a role in the demise in spite of the fact that the quality of the Can-Am marque seemed to be of a level that would sustain the brand for years and years. Sadly it was not to be the case.

Can-Am 175 T'NT Model Highlights

It was the intention of the company from the beginning was to use only the highest quality components.

A powerful motor coupled with light weight made the T'NT and the MX version potent machines at their specific venues.

Plenty of ground clearance and the low saddle height allowed even shorter riders to enjoy the outstanding performance the Can-Am 175 delivered.

A cost of less than $1000 in 1973 helped to pave the way for strong sales in the early years of the new brand.

Fortified fenders resisted breakage like so many others used in the off-road world.

With the T'NT being designated as an endurance model it was complete with lighting and a speedometer for use on the streets.

Powered by a Bombardier engine, the 175 single, two-stroke used a rotary valve to build more power and broaden the power band.

Deemed an enduro model the T'NT was fitted with a speedometer and lighting for use off the unpaved paths.

Typical for the day, the exhaust was finished in matte black and wore a heat shield to protect the rider and mother nature from burns.

Striping on the fenders matched the graphics used on the fuel tank and made for an appealing look.

Motorcycle Specifications:
Can-Am 175 T'NT
Wheelbase: 54 inches
Weight: 222 Pounds (dry)
Seat Height: 30 inches
Displacement: 173.6cc
Gearbox: 5-Speed
Final Drive: Chain
Fuel Delivery: 32mm Bing Concentric Carburetor
Fuel Capacity: 1.9 Gallons
Horsepower: 25@8500 RPM
Top Speed: N/A
MSRP: $ 965
Production: 1973-1982

Motorcycle Ratings:
Available Examples: 1 out of 7
Replacement Parts Availability:
  3 out of 7
Ease of Restoration:
  3 out of 7
Final Value vs Restoration Costs:
  2 out of 7

1982 Can-Am Sonic 500

The Sonic 500 cuts a dramatic pose and was considered a strong competitor in its days of racing

Owner: John Young

The Can-Am brand came to be in 1973 when an engineer named Gary Robinson and World Champion MX rider Jeff Smith decided to build a new class of motorcycle. The new brand would find assistance from the parent company Bombardier who also had a controlling interest in Rotax, makers of engines used in many recreational vehicles. The two founders soldiered on for many years before the Sonic 500 was ready for release.

There were several other competing cycles at the 500cc level, one of which was Honda. When you know you have strong competition prior to taking your first step, you have to bring your best to the table. Checking the specs on the Sonic 500, Can-Am did their homework.

Making its debut as a 1982 model, the Sonic 500 was powered by a 494cc, four cycle Rotax engine that drew life through a Mikuni 36mm carb. Being a four-stroke motor meant smoother delivery of power without the on/off switch of a two-stroke engine.

A pair of Marzocchi 42mm shocks at the front and dual Ohlin dampers at the tail end provided ample performance along with stunning ground clearance. An individual air reservoir was found on each of the front fork legs that allowed the rider to adjust the

The 494cc Rotax powerplant produced 40 horsepower, included a four-valve head of traditional design and used a belt to drive it versus the more common chain.

Much like any off-road cycle, the muffler does double-duty as a spark arrester to reduce the odds of setting the brush aflame during your ride.

The porosity of the plastic used to make the fuel tank permitted the gas to seep out through the pores.

stiffness. The single cylinder motor produced 40 horsepower and the cycle itself weighed only 310 pounds when fueled. A five-speed transmission was aboard and when in fifth gear the Sonic 500 could reach 94 miles per hour. The lighting at both ends meant the Sonic 500 was street legal as well.

Lurking behind the small windscreen the only instrument you find is a tripmeter that can be reset after each run. A small drum brake was found on each hub which was standard equipment in the day. The weight of a disc brake, let alone two was not considered worthwhile in the off-road world. An oversized saddle provided plenty of comfort for the rider but as with most off-road machines a passenger was not an option.

Motorcycle Specifications:
1982 Can-Am Sonic 500
Wheelbase: 58.5 inches
WEIGHT: 310 Pounds (wet)
Seat Height: 38.2 inches
Displacement: 494cc
Gearbox: Five-speed
Final Drive: Chain
Fuel Delivery: 36mm Mikuni Carburetor
Fuel Capacity: 2.6 Gallons
Horsepower: 40
Top Speed: 94 MPH
MSRP: $2999
Production: 1982-1983

Motorcycle Ratings:
Available Examples: 1 out of 7
Replacement Parts Availability:
  2 out of 7
Ease of Restoration:
  2 out of 7
Final Value vs Restoration Costs:
2 out of 7

The business side shows off the powerful Rotax engine's exhaust as well as the final drive chain.

A molded plastic windscreen helped to deflect a few bugs at speed but primarily served to house the headlight and give the resettable trip meter a place to hide.

A magazine review in 1982 showed strong evidence that the Sonic 500 was up to contemporary standards when raced next to a Honda XR500R, one of its most staunch competitors. The Sonic sold for $2999 compared to the Honda's MSRP of $2148 but with only 227 dealers nationwide you did own a bit of exclusivity with the Sonic.

The fuel tank is made of a composite plastic and proved to be rather porous. When fuel was left in the tank for any length of time, the decals applied to the outside would simply fall away from the sides of the tank. Evidence of that process can be seen on this example, although the decals have not fallen completely off yet.

The Sonic 500 was sold in 1982 and 1983, the year that Bombardier decided to license the production to an outside source due to their shift away from motorcycles and related gear. Only four years later, 1987, the Can-Am name would be gone from the market. The brand was later brought back to life with fresh offerings that featured three wheels.

The short lifespan of the company and even shorter life of the Sonic 500 makes finding machines and parts a bit of a challenge. By searching long and hard enough you can find most of the major components but it may be the smaller, detail parts that prove elusive and as always the last 10% of a restoration is the hardest.

1982 Can-Am Sonic 500 Model Highlights

The powerful 494cc Rotax engine is a true gem and delivers plenty of power, regardless of what challenges you throw its way.

Adjustable air pressure at the front forks allows the rider to tailor the ride to the situation.

Quality Ohlins dampers at the tail end offer a variety of adjustments as well.

The saddle is heavily padded but only makes allowance for a rider, not a passenger.

A top speed of 94 miles per hour outpaces most of the other cycle in its class.

With lighting at both front and rear the Sonic is street legal and can be ridden almost anywhere.

1976 CZ Falta 400 Replica

Owner: Norm Carroll

The CZ brand was a Czechoslovakian company that began life in 1932 building motorcycles featuring 73cc, 98cc, 173cc and 248cc engines before the war broke out. After 1945 they returned to production but as a part of the nationalized Czechoslovakian motorcycle industry. Most of their early efforts were aimed at street use but later entries were designed only for off-road events. The Falta 400 Replica was a machine based on the factory works machine of a similar design.

The CZ factory rider, Jaroslav Falta almost won the 1974 world championship but records indicate he actually captured the title but was unfairly treated, thus losing the opportunity. As we've seen elsewhere in this book the replica models closely mimic the factory or works bikes, but with toned down power and equipment. The true works bikes were built in 125cc, 250, and 400cc variations while the replicas only came in 250 and 400 models and were virtually identical. The 400 was also known as a Type 981.

The angular alloy tank was one of the dominant features of the Falta replicas as was the exhaust with the unusual curvature, often called the "snail pipe". The 381cc engine produced 31.6 horsepower at 6000 RPM and had a top speed of 50 MPH. With half a tank of fuel it tipped the scales at 231 pounds and when new it sold for $1670 USD. The unusual lay-down rear shocks were a design detail borrowed from the factory bike and gave the rider a real taste of what the works bike was like to ride. The four-speed gearbox seemed like it was behind the times with most other off-road machines having 5 or 6 speeds on tap. The overall construction of many things from that part of the world in the day was a tad crude, but functional.

Left side of the Falta 400 Replica shows us the "snail pipe" portion of the exhaust which is the short, vertical section just in front of the engine.

Although it features a few unique design features the CZ Falta 400 Replica was a competent machine in its day.

Considering the scarcity of new examples, finding a barn find today would be a rare occurrence. Obviously replacement parts are on the same list and would be a major challenge. Scarcity does not always equate with value so finding one at all won't mean the price should be in the stratosphere, although people can ask what they want.

CZ production continued into the early '80s but then as with so many other motorcycle manufacturers, the competition from the Japanese brands was too much to compete against. The CZ brand can still be seen at shows and events proving the longevity of the most obscure marques.

1976 CZ Falta 400 Replica Model Highlights

The angular alloy tank is one of the more dominant features of the Type 981 and really helps to make it stand out in any crowd.

The unusual "snail pipe" exhaust was another touch that was not found on other machines of its day or before.

The scalloped cylinder head fins are another trait found on the Falta Replica but nowhere else.

Owning a Falta 400 Replica today will set you apart from all the other collectors due to its scarcity.

Motorcycle Specifications:
1976 CZ Falta 400 Replica
Wheelbase: 55.35 in. Weight: 223 Lbs (dry) Seat Height: 34.4 inches
Displacement: 381cc Gearbox: 4-Speed Final Drive: Chain
Fuel Delivery: 33mm Jikov Carburetor
Fuel Capacity: 2.11 Gallons
Horsepower: 31.6@6000
Top Speed: 50 MPH MSRP: $1670
Production: 1974-1976
Motorcycle Ratings:
Available Examples: 1 out of 7
Replacement Parts Availability: 1 out of 7
Ease of Restoration: 1 out of 7
Final Value vs Restoration Costs: 1 out of 7

The angular shape of the alloy fuel tank is an easy way to tell the Falta Replica apart from any similar machines.

The single-cylinder two-stroke displaces 381cc and delivered 31.6 horsepower, making it a staunch competitor on the track.

The oddly cut fins atop the cylinder head are another unique feature found on the Falta Replica.

1970 Ducati 350 Scrambler

The right side shows us the chrome exhaust and another of the soft side covers that actually provided storage.

Asking about the Ducati brand today and you'll get a variety of responses, all of which mention high-end performance on the street and race track. Ducati currently builds some of the most capable machines on the market, but as with so many other firms, in their earlier days produced a much tamer group of machines. Their legendary Desmodromic, V-twin engine resides at the top of the performance list, but it had predecessors that weren't nearly that sexy.

The 1970 350 Scrambler seen here is one that evolved from a long line of modest machines. The 350 Scrambler was first seen as a machine that held a narrow-case engine in its frame and was offered between 1962 and 1967. This example features a wide case engine which made its debut for the 1968 model year. This model ran through 1975 and even before its reign was over Ducati introduced a 450cc variant. Neither the 350 nor 450 were considered to be true super bikes but held their own on tracks as well as city streets. The Ducati single-cylinder engine was replaced by a more potent V-twin for 1973 and pushed Ducati into the next level of performance.

Picking up the pieces after WW II, Ducati rolled out one great machine after another and every iteration saw improvements at every level. With a sibling that displaced 250cc, the 350 Scrambler gained 100cc in

The typical rear suspension uses a pair of coil-over springs finished in chrome.

Displacing 336cc the single used bevel drive to the single overhead non-desmo camshaft. Engine and 5-speed trans are housed in the same case.

the displacement arena as well as a frame built near race machine specs. The 336cc engine was a single-cylinder that was fed by 29mm Dell'Orto carburetion. Power output was above average with a rating of 24 horsepower at 7500 RPM. Weighing 291 pounds dry the 350 Scrambler was also not a light weight but delivered plenty of action whether on the street or your local racing venue. Two gallons of fuel could be placed in the tank which delivered a decent day in the saddle under normal conditions but suffered when the throttle was twisted open.

Unlike other Scramblers on the market the Ducati wore its chrome exhaust pipe low. The tire hugging front fender was typical for many of the machines designed for on and of-road riding at the time and obviously hampered travel when things got muddy. Chrome panels on the sides of the fuel tank were more common on earlier machines, but as used here offset the orange hue nicely.

Basic braking and suspension gave the 350 Scrambler a comfortable ride until you began to push too hard on the overall layout. It didn't boast so much power as to cause trouble so overall it was a great cycle to ride at almost every experience level. The five-speed gearbox was also up to the task but added nothing fresh to the equation. The combination of features, power and looks made the 350 a huge success in the rapidly

A single-downtube frame holds the single-cylinder engine in place and makes a tidy installation.

expanding market that catered to the on and off-road rider.

Ducati 350 Scrambler Model Highlights

The frame was upgraded from previous editions and added rigidity and durability with little weight gain.

The 336cc single-cylinder delivered ample power to suit nearly any riding scenario.

A five-speed gearbox was a part of the design and offered the rider plenty of ratios to meet his needs.

The two-gallon fuel tank didn't provide an excessive range but when taken to the trails its weight was not a deterrent.

A well-padded seat was another way the Ducati provided the rider with all day comfort.

Although mere cosmetics, the chrome side panels and exhaust brought new levels of class to a machine capable of being ridden in the dirt.

Providing the rider with the bare minimum of data the speedometer was easy-to-read when at speed or at rest.

Motorcycle Specifications:
1968-1975 Ducati 350 Scrambler
Wheelbase: N/A
Weight: 291 Pounds (dry)
Seat Height: N/A
Displacement: 336cc
Gearbox: 5-Speed
Final Drive: Chain
Fuel Delivery: 29mm Dell'Orto Carburetor
Fuel Capacity: 2 Gallons
Horsepower: 24@8500 RPM
Top Speed: N/A   **MSRP:** N/A
Production: 1968-1975

Motorcycle Ratings:
Available Examples: 1 out of 7
Replacement Part Availability:
  3 out of 7
Ease of Restoration: 2 out of 7
Final Value vs Restoration Cost:
  2 out of 7

1977 Harley-Davidson MX250

The MX250 was a radical machine for die-hard Harley fans to accept, but the MX machine was certainly well built.

Owner: Illinois Harley-Davidson

Knowing the history of Harley-Davidson as I do, they were seldom afraid of taking a different tack when trying to reach new segments of the market. As anyone in the cycle universe could see, the craze of off-road motorcycle events was gaining speed and momentum in the latter part of the '60s and early '70s. The trend had begun overseas but had reached the shores of the US and was gaining speed. The team at H-D decided to move ahead cautiously as off-road machines were not exactly their bailiwick. Four years after beginning the research and design work, a group of 100 MX250s were sent to dealers in the expansive network that is Harley-Davidson.

The early machines were fitted with unusual suspension at both ends and didn't draw much attention from buyers, at least not the good kind. For the 1977 model year a fresher version was offered for sale, a version that was better received by dealers and buyers alike. The MX250 was not built in any of Harley's factories, but assembled in Italy by their Italian partners at Aermacchi. A large number of earlier models had hailed from the same facility or at least the motors came from the same plant. To power the new machine a 249cc single cylinder engine was installed in a chrome-moly frame. The chosen technology was on

Oversized graphics on the tank told the world what you were riding a genuine Harley.

Molded in bright orange, the plastic the tank held 2.2 gallons of fuel and was kept in place by a leather strap.

The prototype of the MX250 had an unconventional suspension setup at the back end which was replaced with a more traditional arrangement for production, as seen on this example.

par with the market in the day so we can at least give H-D credit for trying to take on this new venture with the proper gear. The MX250 weighed a respectably light 247 pounds when half-fueled and a 38mm Dell 'Orto carb fed the two-stroke engine with ease. Power output was not stated in the day but from looking at the stats it should have fallen within the range of most other machines of the period.

Timing for a new product is crucial to success and Harley's could not have been worse. By the time the '77 models were rolling into dealers' showrooms, they were doing the same at Honda, Suzuki, Kawasaki and Yamaha dealers across the US.

Though the Harley's performance might have been similar to that of the metric brands, the price was not. The MX250 retailed for $1695 while the bikes from Japan sold for less. The higher price, combined with the fact that most buyers didn't equate the Milwaukee brand with motocross machines, meant that the end came swiftly. 1978 was the final year of sale for the MX250 and I can find no production figures for either year they were built.

Much like some of Harley's attempts at selling models outside of their comfort zone, the MX250 was designed and built well but there was never enough of an audience for the bike to survive in a highly competitive market dominated by the Japanese brands.

Beautiful examples of the MX250 can be seen on display at museums with an occasional example seen at a swap meet. Overall, the MX has become even more of a recluse now than when they were new. A few online listings for the MX250 can be found, but the prices seem to be a tad unrealistic. Again, with so few manufactured a person can ask what they want. Getting their price is another story altogether. A fair amount of parts auctions can be found on eBay so returning a copy to its former glory

Like many two-stroke competition engines of the day, the Aermacchi 242cc engine was fitted with an expansion chamber designed for optimum performance.

Much like every other MX machine being sold, the MX250 was brought to life with a kick-start lever.

may not be impossible, just don't expect it to be easy.

Harley-Davidson MX250 Model Highlights

As stated earlier, the MX250 was well built and featured to a level on par with the competition.

A chrome-moly frame was rigid enough to handle the terrain.

The Aermacchi engine displaced 243cc and was in line with engines used in other models on the market. Were it not for the staunch competition they faced from the Japanese offerings the MX250 could have easily been one of Harley's greatest.

Motorcycle Specifications:
1977-1978 Harley-Davidson MX250
Wheelbase: 58 inches
Weight: 247 Pounds (1/2 tank of fuel)
Seat Height: 36.3 inches
Displacement: 242.6 cc
Gearbox: 5-Speed
Final Drive: Chain
Fuel Delivery: 38mm Dell 'Orto Carburetor
Fuel Capacity: 2.2 Gallons
Horsepower: N/A
Top Speed: N/A
MSRP: $1695
Production: 1977-1978

Motorcycle Ratings:
Available Examples:
1 out of 7
Replacement Part Availability:
3 out of 7
Ease of Restoration: 3 out of 7
Final Value vs Restoration Costs:
4 out of 7

1973 Harley-Davidson SR-100

The Italian firm of Aermacchi provided the 98cc engine used in the SR-100 as well as many other Harleys of the period in a variety of smaller displacements.

Owner: Norm Carroll

As some of us may recall, the late '60s and early '70s presented many opportunities to stray from the norm of the day. People were trying all sorts of new things and as a company with 70 years of history, Harley-Davidson also experimented with some non-typical motorcycle options. Their use of Aermacchi engines in a number of smaller Harleys was done in hopes of drawing in riders who were put off by the full size models from H-D, or who simply wanted a simpler machine.

As mentioned in an earlier entry, in 1977 Harley brought out it's first full-size, off-road motorcycle, the MX-250, which in turn failed after only two years. Prior to that launch and dismal failure a handful of simpler "off-road" models were shown at local dealers. The SR-100 was one of those attempts and wasn't too bad a machine, all things considered. The Japanese makers were sending a wide range of small and easy to ride models to the USA and H-D hoped to snag a few of those buyers with an offering from Milwaukee.

Based on a tubular steel frame, the SR-100 held a 98cc, single-cylinder, two-stroke engine in its flanks. A single Dell 'Orto concentric carburetor fed the fuel and air mix as needed, power was delivered to the rear wheel through a five-speed gearbox. With a wheelbase of only 52 inches the SR-100 was compact if nothing else. Ceriani type forks at the front and coil-over shocks at the rear gave the SR-100 a decent ride and ground clearance of 10.8 inches, which was more than enough for the casual off-road rider. The Harley-Davidson literature of the time stated that the SR-100, "took the Mexican 1000 and Baja 500" but there were no further bragging rights listed.

A weight of 212 pounds is shown but no mention of whether that figure was wet or dry, but since the tank only holds 2.5 gallons you wouldn't add a lot of weight if it was full. A 21 inch diameter tire up front was joined by a 18 incher out back. The saddle height was a bit of a reach for shorter riders at 34 inches. A drum brake measuring 5.305 inches was mounted to each hub to slow the diminutive machine to a halt. Fitted with a headlight and tail light, the SR-100 could be ridden on the street as well as the dirt, although a complete lack of instrumentation made your speed a guessing game.

The SR-100 was never able to get any traction with the buyers in the USA and was only sold for two years. By that time the Japanese were bringing in better and better machines to conquer the dirt - and people who bought Harley-Davidsons didn't think of the brand when shopping for a light weight off-road model. The poor sales when new reflect on the examples found today, and that is a scant few. There seem to be a decent supply of parts on the open market and maybe as many at the swap meet level, but that is often a crap shoot.

Harley-Davidson SR-100 Model Highlights

The SR-100 presented the rider with a nice set of features including light weight and ample power

Weighing only 200 pounds before fuel,

A polished metal fender helped to keep the big chunks off of the rider and helped to protect the headlight from damage as well.

Born in the days when Harley-Davidson was owned by AMF this style of graphics were used on nearly every model in the catalog.

The exhaust system included a perforated steel heat shield and a spark arrester, all of it finished in black.

the SR-100 was no problem to ride or park when the time came.

The compact engine hailed from Aermacchi in Italy which may have irked some loyal Harley fans but the Motor Company had nothing of its type in their own parts bin.

The small drum brake at each end of the chassis was enough to slow the tiny machine down from speed.

The simplicity of the design and layout made the SR-100 an easy choice for many first time riders assuming their legs were long enough

Using the engine as a stressed-member of the chassis helped saved weight.

The left side of the SR-100 shows us the upswept exhaust and high-mounted muffler.

Motorcycle Specifications: 1973-1974 Harley-Davidson SR-100	
Wheelbase: 52 inches	**Horsepower:** N/A
Weight: 212 Pounds	**Top Speed:** N/A **MSRP:** N/A
Seat Height: 34 inches	**Production:** 1973 and 1974
Displacement: 98cc	
Gearbox: 5-Speed	**Motorcycle Ratings:**
Final Drive: Chain	**Available Examples:** 1 out of 7
Fuel Delivery: Dell'Orto Carburetor	**Replacement Part Availability:** 3 out of 7
Fuel Capacity: 2.5 Gallons	**Ease of Restoration:** 2 out of 7
	Final Value vs Restoration Cost: 2 out of 7

1977 Hodaka 250 Thunder Dog

Owner: Rex Cusumano

By the time the 1977 Hodaka models were introduced the company was nearing its end, but didn't know that yet. While sales were OK the competition grew more competitive every day and even brand loyalty only goes so far. Hodaka was even having trouble holding on to their factory race riders as they too were lured away to the bigger players in the game.

The Hodaka 250 was also known as Thunder Dog and followed in the footsteps of its smaller sibling the Super Combat 125 that made its debut in 1974. The Thunder Dog had a displacement of double that found in the Super Combat at 246cc. The engine featured a new technique that Hodaka called "alumiferric" and consisted of casting aluminum fins around an iron cylinder core, the claimed results were better cooling, and improved performance along with reduced weight. At the core of the design the engine was still a two-stroke with a 5-speed gearbox. A 36mm Mikuni carb was chosen to deliver the proper blend of fuel and air into the cylinders so the Thunder Dog was sure to have plenty of power.

When filled with every ounce of fuel the 2-1/2 gallon vessel could hold, the Thunder Dog tipped the scales at a svelte 268 pounds. The previous trend for Hodakas was to have a chrome plated fuel tank but the Super Combat ended that with a tank molded in Hodaka Orange. The Thunder Dog continued that tradition and added a pair of Preston Petty fenders in the same hue. The 250 provided 9 inches of ground clearance which also came as a benefit to the rider who was taking on more aggressive courses. The seat height was listed at

The classic Hodaka orange became an integral part of the molded fuel tank and fenders, which were products of the Preston Petty company a supplier of plastic fenders to many riders.

The Hodaka 250 checked off all the boxes when shopping for a true race machine that looked the part.

33-1/2 inches which was moderate for most machines of the day, especially for bigger displacement models. Literature didn't list horsepower, only the engine speed at which maximum power was achieved, 7000 RPM.

The Thunder Dog 250 also came with a Preston Petty trail lighting kit that could be easily affixed to the motorcycle if riding after dark was a part of your plans. In 1978, Shell which was the parent company, was reviewing their books and noticed that the division handling Hodaka was losing money, a lot of it, and chose to kill the Hodaka line. It had been a good run for the spunky maker with unusual names but the brand retains a loyal following with an annual gathering that draws 1000s of people and their Hodaka cycles.

1977 Hodaka Thunder Dog 250 Model Highlights

The improved power provided by the 246cc engine gave the 250 a real boost and was considered to be a great machine at a lower cost.

Preston Petty fenders were more durable than those used earlier on Hodakas.

The bike is a nice combination of light weight and good power output.

Nine inches of ground clearance meant there weren't too many places the Thunder Dog couldn't be ridden.

Hodaka's "Alumiferric" technology used for the cylinders claimed to create a cooler running, better performing engine.

The molded fuel tank that replaced the earlier chrome plated metal version, first seen on the Super Combat, was a welcome change continued on the 250 Thunder Dog.

The single-cylinder mill in the Thunder Dog displaced 244cc and delivered a great amount of bang for the money.

Stifling sound, and protecting the elements from sparks were all parts of the design for any good off-road muffler.

Motorcycle Specifications:
1977 Hodaka 250 Thunder Dog
Wheelbase: 57 in.   Weight:
245 Pounds (dry)   Seat Height: 33.5 in.
Displacement: 246cc
Gearbox: 5-Speed
Final Drive: Chain
Fuel Delivery: 36mm Mikuni Carburetor
Fuel Capacity: 2.5 Gallons
Horsepower: N/A   Top Speed: N/A
MSRP: N/A

Motorcycle Ratings:
Available Examples: 2 out of 7
Availability of Replacement Parts:
  3 out of 7
Ease of Restoration: 3 out of 7
Final Value vs Restoration Costs:
3 out of 7

1971 Hodaka Ace 100B

There's no way to disguise the tiny dimensions of the Ace B, but it provided fun way beyond what its size suggested.

Owner: Rex Cusumano

Hodaka had its first efforts nearly come to a certain end in the late '60s but the brand was resurrected a few years later. As we know the market for off-road machines was expanding rapidly in that period and Hodaka sold a line of lower cost models that still performed like a more expensive machine. With models named the Combat Wombat and Dirt Squirt you could tell there was something different about the brand and what it offered.

The Hodaka Ace was their first effort and powered by only a 90cc engine it did have some shortcomings. Small displacement motorcycles weren't new so the Hodaka still found a niche among buyers. At the end of the '60s Hodaka had begun honing their machines for specific riding styles in an effort to keep up with demand and increasing competition for overseas. Based on the Ace 100, the Super Rat was an MX version aimed at that style of racing. The Ace 100B had already proven itself to be a competent machine that was easy to ride and offered plenty of fun for the price.

Equipped with lights at both ends, a speedometer up front and a chrome luggage rack at the rear the Ace 100B served many masters and gave a lot of people their

The blacked-out exhaust was fitted with a chrome heat shield and exhaust tip for longer life.

The 98cc two-stroke engine cradled in the Ace B frame was adequate for the size of the cycle.

Providing a place to store small items, the chrome plated rack was another convenience that most other machines in this class lacked.

first experience on two-wheels. Advertising for the Ace 100B claimed that three out of four Hodaka owners tried the competition first, and then rode home on a Hodaka. Other claims touted the 183 pound weight and greater horsepower at lower RPM. A CYCLE GUIDE magazine review in November of 1970 said "It would be difficult to find fault with this red/chrome wonder". Further claims of quality and durability did nothing to hinder sales and the quirky brand flourished even in a world of intense competition.

Construction of the 100B was sturdy and used the first full down-tube frame in the industry. 11 inches of ground clearance let you take on any trail and the 2-3/4 gallon fuel tank helped extend your fun. The chrome plated fenders resisted chipping compared to pained versions but rough conditions did bring on bending.

The Super Rat was the more extreme version of the 100B and was aimed at the MX segment of the market. Built for a higher degree of rugged riding it too won races and the hearts and check books of buyers. Hodaka did its best to introduce fresh models to entice buyers with grater displacement engines their catalog grew but not their list of buyers. By 1978 the competition from other makers turned out to be too much for the Hodaka line to continue. In its wake it has left us with a fairly expansive pool of retired machines and plenty of parts to return them to original condition. The cost of doing so will be far lower than restoring most other machines of the day and will still be great fun to ride when you're done.

1971 Hodaka Ace 100 B Model Highlights

Ease of operation and low cost of entry were two of Hodaka's strong suits.

The inexpensive machines were well built and delivered plenty of power to the entry level racer.

Chrome plating on the tank and fenders resisted chipping like painted versions and looked great too.

Weighing only 183 pounds the 100 B was easy to ride around town or the local off-road trails.

The MSRP was right around $500 and for the time provided a lot of bang for your buck.

The rubber extensions on the metal fenders added a small measure of protection and allowed the chrome to last a little longer.

The chrome tank gleams in the afternoon sun and calls its rider to climb aboard.

Motorcycle Specifications:
1971 Hodaka Ace 100 B
Wheelbase: 52.36 inches
Weight: 183 Pounds (dry)
Seat Height: 32 inches
Displacement: 98cc
Gearbox: 5-Speed
Final Drive: Chain
Fuel Delivery: 26mm Mikuni Carburetor
Fuel Capacity: 2-3/4 Gallons
Horsepower: N/A

Top Speed: N/A
MSRP: Approx. $500

Motorcycle Ratings:
Available Examples: 3 out of 7
Availability of Replacement Parts:
  4 out of 7
Ease of Restoration: 4 out of 7
Final Value vs Restoration Costs:
  4 out of 7

1974 Hodaka Super Rat 100

The low-slung exhaust was out of character for an off-road machine but did help to keep the center of gravity low.

Owner: Rex Cusumano

The Hodaka brand came to be in 1964 when the factory that built the Yamaguchi motorcycles in Japan closed its doors. An American named Henry Koepke began production of his new brand soon after in the same facility. Distribution in the USA was handled by Pabatco (Pacific Based Trading Company) the same year as production began. The Hodaka marque would go on to offer several small off-road machines, many of which cam with unusual names - Wombat, Combat Wombat and the Super Rat among them.

The Super Rat was only the second production model offered by Hodaka and followed the Ace 90. The Super Rat was powered by a slightly larger 100cc engine that was fed with a 28mm Mikuni carb and sparked via a CDI ignition. Hodaka had a unique process called "Alumiferric" (mentioned in another listing) that resulted in an modern and somewhat unique cylinder that promised lighter weight and enhanced cooling.

The Super Rat was built to a design that resulted in a low center of gravity which enabled the rider to perform at levels of higher grade machines. Even the exhaust was mounted lower on the chassis than many other off-road models. The 21 inch front wheel also aided in the handling department, especially when coupled to the low weight of the Super Rat. As an option you could buy a road kit that allowed you to modify your Super Rat for street use whereas the original layout was pure race machine.

The Super Rat was sold between the years 1970 and 1977 and the early models were dressed with chrome tanks, a red frame and featured a large, cylindrical air cleaner on the side of the engine that wore the "Super Rat" graphics. By the time 1974 rolled around, Hodaka and every other manufacturer were feeling the pressure from Honda. The CR125 and CR250 Elsinore models were the primary reason for the feelings of pressure and Hodaka chose to ramp up the Super Rat to compete.

One of Hodaka's selling points from the beginning was the low cost of admission. The Super Rat had an MSRP of $499 when it made its debut for 1970 and that fact alone helped them sell a lot of machines in the USA. The fact that they were pretty good motorcycles for that amount didn't hurt them either, but even a low cost can't keep away all of the competition. For the 1974 edition the Super Rat Hodaka improved several items on the machine and radically altered its appearance. Gone was the chrome tank, red frame and oversized air cleaner. The newest version still carried a reduced MSRP but now looked the part of a more serious candidate in the MX arena. The dark blue frame was offset by the bright orange tank and fenders and a more traditional air cleaner was used to save weight and improve function.

Sadly there was little Hodaka could do to maintain a competitive edge. As men-

The 100cc two-stroke engine provided the Super Rat with adequate power and permitted neophyte riders a chance to get interested in the sport of MX racing.

A popular upgrade for the Super Rat was a fork brace that helped keep the fork legs rigid under tough riding conditions.

The revised colors and trim on the 1974 gave the Super Rat a more menacing look which was one of the company's goals.

A typical upgrade in the day was to replace the standard rear shocks with units that provided more control and adjustments like these from WorksPerformance.

Supplanting the chrome edition of the fuel tanks happened for the 1974 Super Rat as Hodaka tried to combat the attack from Honda's Elsinore models.

tioned before, Hodaka was part of a larger firm, Shell. Continuing financial losses brought about the end. The year 1978 was the last year of operation for Hodaka.

Today's market isn't flooded with parts for the brand, but the popularity of the early models remains high as collectors and fans gather to celebrate the legacy of Hodaka.

Hodaka Super Rat Model Highlights

The MSRP of the original Super Rat was only $499 and allowed a lot of people entry to the new world of off-road racing.

A low center of gravity made the Super Rat an easier cycle to ride than others on the market and helped give beginning riders more confidence.

Many fans of the brand always liked the odd names used for the different models. Hard to argue with Combat Wombat and Dirt Squirt.

Several well-known companies sold parts to enhance the performance of the Hodaka machines, the Super Rat included.

Replacement parts are still available today which permits almost anyone to own and restore their Hodaka to factory fresh conditions.

Motorcycle Specifications:
1974 Hodaka Super Rat
Wheelbase: N/A
Weight: N/A
Seat Height: N/A
Displacement: 100cc
Gearbox: 5-Speed
Final Drive: Chain
Fuel Delivery: 28mm Mikuni Carburetor
Fuel Capacity: N/A
Horsepower: N/A
Top Speed: N/A
MSRP: $499
Production: 1970-1977

Motorcycle Ratings:
Available Examples: 2 out of 7
Replacement Part Availability:
  4 out of 7
Ease of Restoration: 3 out of 7
Final Value vs Restoration Cost:
  2 out of 7

1962 Honda CL72

Owner: Roger Smith

The universe of off-road motorcycles contains a wide array of variations on the theme. There are hard core MX machines at one end and more user friendly, family oriented models like the scrambler on the other. By definition a scrambler was designed for use whether on road or off but when the pavement ended the capabilities of most scramblers grew limited in nature. The tire hugging front fenders and primarily street tread tires put a strain on any off-road action. The high mounted exhaust told a different tale.

Honda built a dizzying number of CL editions, otherwise known as their scrambler series. The 1962s were the first of their kind from Honda but would certainly not be the last. They were often based on a true street legal machine with a set of high pipes attached. As long as your off-road riding plans didn't include any ISDT or MX events you could ride in the dirt at your father's farm or wander down a timid trail. But beyond that you were asking for trouble aboard a CL. Off road adventures tended to take a toll on both rider and machines with any number of bends and breaks occurring. This example of the CL72 wears an alloy fuel tank which was a Honda produced item built in very limited numbers. Only 113 of them were produced and the thickness of the fuel tank walls is so thin you could dent it with a stern glance. Knowing this its doubtful that anyone owning one would venture off the pavement unless they had a second copy of the scarce tank in their garage.

With the exception of the rare fuel tank this CL72 is as factory as Honda made them, restored to better than delivered standards. Being the first year ever for the scrambler design, the scrambler would see

The high-mounted exhaust was the trademark of a scrambler even if none of the other hardware would suit off-road action.

A set of beefy tires gave the CL72 a great ride on the pavement but lacked the real added traction required for semi-serious off-road riding.

changes in subsequent model years. A twin-cylinder, four-cycle engine displacing 247cc was hung in the frame. Fed by a pair of 28mm Keihin carbs the little twin developed a whopping 24 horsepower. Weighing 337 pounds before adding fuel, the CL was sprightly on the streets but the bulk would quickly become an obstacle on the dirt or trails.

The scrambler layout was not unique to Honda and soon the market was littered with a varying supply of machines that claimed on and off road abilities. The others tended to be overly optimistic regarding the playing in the dirt skills but hoped to expand their sales by shouting those claims to the market. Examples of Hondas CL models can be found with relative ease considering how many of them were imported into the USA between 1962 and 1965. Finding one with the alloy tank is another story but for a great all-around cycle you'd be hard pressed to do better than a CL from Honda.

1962 Honda CL72 Model Highlights

Easy to buy and easy to ride are two strong attributes of the CL72 from Honda.

The kick-start only was intended to give the rider a feel of being a real biker and luckily for them the CL started without too much trouble.

A top speed of 74 MPH means you can ride the CL72 on the highway but caution would be needed today with higher posted limits and drivers who often exceed them.

Sources for parts are plentiful for Honda and very few items are hard to find with most available with a few clicks of the mouse.

The saddle is long and well-padded and a set of passenger foot pegs means you can bring a friend along on your adventure.

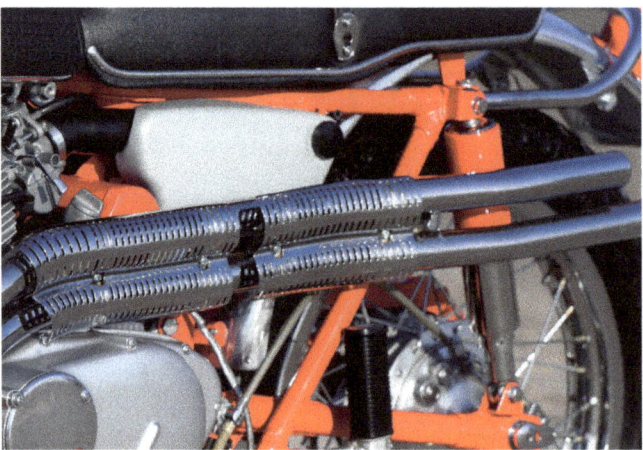

The ubiquitous heat shield helped give the CL that ready-for-off-road look.

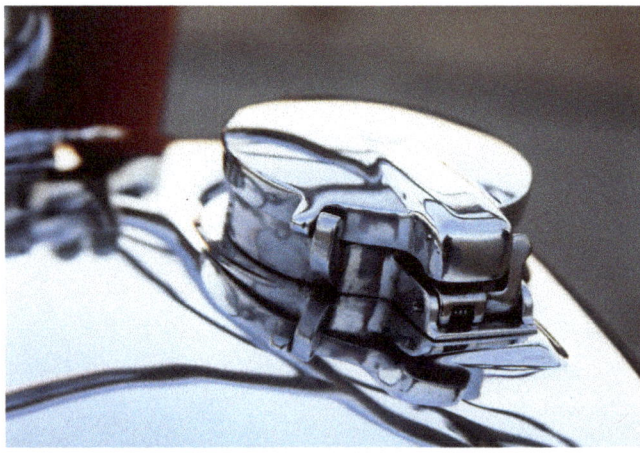

Not only is the alloy tank a rarity, the exotic fuel caps found on the alloy models were often torn off and replaced with a more traditional style.

Motorcycle Specifications:
1962 Honda CL72
 Wheelbase: 52.4 in.
Weight: 337 Pounds (dry)
Seat Height: N/A
Displacement: 247cc
Gearbox: 4-Speed   **Final Drive:** Chain
Fuel Delivery: (2) 28mm Keihin Carburetors
Fuel Capacity: 2.8 Gallons
Horsepower: 24@9500 RPM
Top Speed: 74 MPH   **MSRP:** N/A

Motorcycle Ratings
Available Examples: 3 out of 7
Availability of Replacement Parts:
  4 out of 7
Ease of Restoration: 3 out of 7
Final Value vs Restoration Costs:
  3 out of 7

1974 Honda CR-125M Elsinore

Honda's reduced version of the CR-250M was an overnight success in 1974 and remains a popular choice today for collectors and riders.

Owner: Rex Cusumano

By the time the 1974 model year had come into view the off-road craze had developed a wide following. Riders craved better machines to take to tracks that were springing up around the country. As with many forms of motor sports the movement already had a strong group of enthusiasts overseas before the action reached U.S. shores. For the previous year Honda debuted their CR-250M to the stateside market. Named the Elsinore after a famous California event held at Lake Elsinore, the new machine showcased several new features for a Honda and really added to its mystique and value. Early examples were found to be kind of delicate for serious off-road efforts and many components proved to be too fragile to survive a weekend of fun. On top of that, many smaller riders who were just getting started found the CR-250M a bit too big and powerful.

To combat both issues Honda created the CR-125M and released it to the dealer network in the latter part of 1973. The reduced-size model carried a 123cc, single-cylinder engine in its flanks that was of the 2-stroke design. A 6-speed gearbox supplanted the 5-speed used on the 250 variant and overall the CR-125M weighed 34 pounds less before adding fuel and fluids. The saddle height was slightly lower than the 250's and the fuel tank held 1.6 gallons versus 1.8 in the 250.

The popularity and success of the smaller off-road machine was immediate and would soon become one of Honda's best-selling motorcycles. The MSRP of $749 played a role in that as did the improved durability and reduced dimensions. The smaller engine was lighter than the 250 and part of that equation came from the use of magnesium alloy for the crank case. This element was quite strong yet very lightweight. At 8500 RPM the CR-125M produced nearly 17 horsepower which was more than adequate although you had to keep the motor spinning at the upper end of the RPM range to get that performance.

A chrome-moly steel, tubular frame delivered a high degree of rigidity while again, saving weight. The front forks provided more than seven inches of ground clearance which is also a criterion for any successful off-road mount. The first-year CR-125Ms wore a polished silver tank with "expert green" highlights on the top of the fuel tank. Both fenders were painted silver while sporting green number plates. Being a true off-road model the CR-125M bore no lighting at either end.

CR-125M Model Highlights

The reduction is size from the CR-250M proved to make the CR-125M a nimble machine that could be ridden by nearly anyone.

The six-speed gearbox allowed the rider enough ratios to keep the smaller Honda in the sweet spot of the smaller horsepower rating.

Lighter weight also played a role in the success among smaller riders while still delivering plenty of power and comfort.

With an MSRP of only $749 in 1975, ownership of a CR-125 was open to nearly any budget.

The single-cylinder, 123cc engine delivered plenty of power to the 180 pound CR and really added to the entertainment equation.

A fairly typical addition for any off-road machine, the handlebars were fitted with a foam pad on the cross bar to reduce injury to the rider in case of a fall.

A common alteration for the CR-125M was the upgraded rear shocks to enhance comfort and performance. This set hails from Works Performance.

The first edition CR-125s sported a 1.6 gallon fuel tank that was finished in Custom Silver Metallic paint with Expert Green accents.

Despite its smaller size the CR-125M provided riders of all ages a great performance at a price point that made it easy to buy.

Based on the fairly long production cycle and its popularity, locating parts for your own CR-125M won't be as challenging as it is many other motorcycles.

As soon as the CR-125M was introduced, riders began winning more than their fair share of trophies and it forced nearly all other makers to reconsider their plans.

The popularity of the CR models makes it easier finding parts today than for some other machines of the period.

Additional power came from the use of a DG Exhaust and extra protection from the skid plate seen below the engine.

Motorcycle Specifications:
1974-1978 Honda CR-125M
Wheelbase: 53.5 inches
Weight (dry): 180 Pounds
Seat Height: 32.3 inches
Displacement: 123cc
Gearbox: 6-Speed
Final Drive: Chain
Fuel Delivery: 32mm Mikuni Carburetor
Fuel Capacity: 1.6 Gallons
Horsepower: 17@8500 RPM

Top Speed: N/A
MSRP: $749
Production: 1974-1978

Motorcycle Ratings:
Available Examples: 3 out of 7
Replacement Parts Availability:
  5 out of 7
Ease of Restoration: 3 out of 7
Final Value vs Restoration Cost:
  2 out of 7

1972 Honda XL250 Motosport

Owner: Rex Cusumano

Anyone even vaguely familiar with the Honda brand knows they earned a reputation for designing and producing numerous trend setting machines. In the world of off-road cycles the XL250 Motosport is ranked among the best. Capable of use both on and off-road, the 250 Motosport was an amazing creation that remains high on the list of collectors today.

Cradled in the steel tubular frame we find a 248cc, single-cylinder, four-stroke engine that includes a four-valve layout. A majority of machines built in this era were powered by a two-stroke motor but Honda chose the four-stroke to permit smooth operation whether riding the trails or the streets. The four-stroke design used on this model also permitted easier starting than most of the two-stroke variants and also delivered 20 horsepower to the rider. A 28mm Keihin carburetor was on hand to mete out the precise amount of fuel and did an admirable job at its task. It utilized a push-pull design that was found on street machines and delivered accurate function whether accelerating or slowing down. Under the seat you find a wet polyurethane foam filter that allows clean air to flow to the engine with little or no restriction. A five-speed gearbox was installed and was the most common feature found on the 250 Motosport.

The smooth engine and comfortable ride made the 250 Motosport a popular choice for the two years it was offered.

The high-mounted exhaust and muffler can be seen on this side of the 250 Motosport. Custom Silver Metallic paint with red accents still looks great today.

The 56 inch wheelbase was a tad longer than many other cycles of the period but provided comfortable riding on the street without adding too much grief on unpaved surfaces. 7-1/2 inches of ground clearance allowed the 250 Motosport to traverse fairly aggressive terrain while keeping the saddle height to a distance of 32.3 inches off the tarmac.

Weight when the 2.2 gallon tank was half full was 278 pounds which was also considered a great feature of the XL250. The combination exhaust, spark-arrester and heat shield were mounted high on the frame to reduce the chance of setting brush fires when on the open trail and displayed the "250 Motosport" badge proudly. Capable of attaining a top speed of 80 miles per hour the Motosport provided the rider with adequate performance for nearly any day-to-day activity. The width of the handlebars measured 33 inches and gave the rider plenty of leverage on the open trails or on the roads on the way back home.

A 21 inch hoop up front was joined by a smaller 18 inch model at the rear and both hubs had a small drum brake as part of their construction. The hubs were conical, which was another method of saving weight, while delivering more than adequate function. A telescopic fork at the front was joined by a pair of coil spring shocks at the rear, a ream that worked well on or off road. Final drive was via a single-row chain, another of the more common features of the 250 Motosport.

The Custom Silver Metallic paint was applied to the tank and fenders as was the accent stripes of deep red. The saddle was a comfortable perch for one or two riders although double-up riding reduced performance drastically. A speedometer and tachometer were found atop the triple-tree and was an item not usually found on most dual-purpose machines.

About the only drawback of the 250 Motosport today is finding an example to restore. With only two years of production to its name very few examples can be found on the market now. For the same reason, locating the required parts will take some extra sleuthing that will take you beyond the usual online or swap-meet sources.

Fitted with both speedometer and tachometer the 250 Motosport was one the best equipped off-road machines on the market at the time.

Displacing 248cc and using the four-stroke design helped to set the 250 Motosport apart from other similar offerings of the period.

Well-padded and big enough for two, the seat on the XL250 was only 32.3 inches off the street, making it an easier choice for some shorter riders.

Combing the muffler, spark arrester and heat shield made the unit on the XL250 one of the more efficient designs found in 1972.

Mounted high enough to permit plenty of off-road adventures the front fender was finished in the same color as the fuel tank.

250 Motosport Model Highlights

A combination of easy starting and comfortable ride made the 250 Motosport a great choice for both street and off-road buyers.

The four-stroke engine delivered plenty of power at whisper-quiet sound levels making the Honda a machine that would offend no one.

Full instrumentation gave the rider far more input than many other machines of the same ilk.

Drum brakes at both ends provided adequate stopping power for the trails and was OK for street use too.

Weighing in at less than 300 pounds made the 250 Motosport capable of traversing off-road surfaces without bogging the rider down.

Listed as a dual-purpose model the 250 Motosport also carried both head and tail lights.

Both tires were of the knobby design but were not so aggressive as to thwart street riding while still providing adequate of traction when taken off road.

Motorcycle Specifications:
1972-1973 Honda 250 Motosport
Wheelbase: 56 inches
Weight: 278 Pounds (1/2 tank of fuel)
Seat Height: 32.3 inches
Displacement: 248cc
Gearbox: 5-speed
Final Drive: Chain
Fuel Delivery: 28mm Keihin Carburetor
Fuel Capacity: 2.2 Gallons
Horsepower: 20@8000 RPM
Top Speed: Approx. 80 MPH
MSRP: N/A
Production: 1972 and 1973

Motorcycle Ratings:
Available Examples: 1 out of 7
Replacement Part Availability: 2 out of 7
Ease of Restoration: 2 out of 7
Final Value vs Restoration Cost: 2 out of 7

1970 Kawasaki F21M

Being one of the earliest "motocross" designs offered to the US market, the F21M has become a coveted classic that is rarely seen in original condition, if at all.

Owner: Gary Lingbeck

Kawasaki introduced the F21M as a 1968 model and it was one of the earliest examples of a true off-road machine. Honda didn't debut the Elsinore until 1973 and Suzuki had a similar machine appear in the latter part of the '70s. A simple configuration didn't take anything away from the potency of the F21M. With a 238cc single that produced 30 horsepower with only 225 pounds to move the F21 was fun at any speed.

When first seen it wore a red fuel tank that was adorned with the winged logo of earlier Kawasaki models and a rubber knee pad on either side of the tank. For 1969 and 1970 the lime green and white color scheme was applied and the "green streak" moniker was created. From its inception the F21M carried a silver engine in the frame and used a black exhaust system and alloy fenders. Riders found these delicate items to be a bit too sensitive and many replaced them with plastic ones soon after their first ride and fall. A 26mm Mizuki carb fed the single-cylinder, Kawasaki's rotary-valve design helped to smooth out the torque curve of the two-cycle engine. A four speed transmission was pretty standard equipment at the time as were the small drum brakes on both the front and rear wheels.

The torque and horsepower generated from the single-cylinder two-cycle engine was impressive for the day and for its small size.

The factory installed steering damper was a unique feature of the F21M and would be seldom seen on off-road models in the future.

With plastic fenders still being a few years in the future the alloy variations used on the F21M looked great but were easily bent and broken.

The wheelbase was compact at 53 inches, with a full 9 inches of ground clearance the Kawasaki could handle some pretty rugged terrain. Coil spring shocks at the rear and a hydraulic front fork were typical, but the steering damper was a unique feature that came as a stock item. Weighing 225 pounds before fluids was again a typical number for the F21M. When ridden, however, the bike itself proved to be anything but typical, and was indeed a premier motorcycle at the time.

Production of the F21M ran from 1968 to 1970, the total number built is unknown. Regardless, finding a copy today will not be an easy task. The odds of finding one as clean as the one seen here are slim to none. By design these machines weren't meant to be decorations in your garage, but to be taken out and ridden hard, which they often were with the expected damage and short life expectancy.

A well-padded saddle was a nice place to spend an afternoon, this example has been fitted with a set of buddy pegs, because the original owner liked taking his kids for rides on the back. Beyond that this example is 100% original including paint and fenders.

Overall the scarcity of these models would make selecting it as your next project bike a less than desirable choice. Searching modern web sites showed a bare minimum of options for finding replacement parts.

F21M Model Highlights

The rugged nature of the design made the F21M a great choice for someone hoping to get started in competition.

Power was rated at 30 horsepower and for a machine of such small dimensions that really made for some excitement.

When full of fuel the F21M still weighed less than 250 pounds, which only added to the thrills of off-road riding.

The simplicity of the design made it easy to ride regardless of your experience and made it more appealing to the novice rider.

The alloy fenders looked great but sadly didn't usually last beyond the first contact with the hard ground.

Nine inches of ground clearance made the F21M a capable machine in serious conditions and the torque of the engine was another positive trait.

Kawasaki's rotary-valve technology delivered enhanced performance for two-stroke engines available at the time.

The lime green and white paint replaced the red seen on the 1968 models and was referred to as the "green streak".

The physical layout of the F21M didn't change during its three year production and the upswept exhaust always kept the earth safe from the heat.

Motorcycle Specifications:
Wheelbase: 53 inches
Weight: 225 Pounds (dry)
Seat Height: N/A
Displacement: 238cc
Gearbox: 4-Speed
Final Drive: Chain
Fuel Delivery: 26mm Mizuki Carburetor
Fuel Capacity: 1.9 Gallons
Horsepower: 30@7000 RPM
Top Speed: N/A

MSRP: $865
Production: 1968-1970

Motorcycle Ratings:
Available Examples: 1 out of 7
Replacement Part Availability:
  1 out of 7
Ease of Restoration: 1 out of 7
Final Value vs Restoration Cost:
  4 out of 7

1974 Kawasaki F7 175

Owner: Greg Lingbeck

The duties of a dual-purpose motorcycle are a bit more adventurous than that of a pure street or off-road model as they needed to serve two masters with equal dexterity. A wide variety of said machines have been on the market since the late '60s and those coming to market in the early '70s were assuming a more sophisticated set of skills for the off-road enthusiast.

The Kawasaki F7 was first sold as a 1971 model and would continue until 1975 when it was supplanted by another variant. In contrast to many of the earlier versions, the F7 carried its front fender high enough to permit some semi-serious off-road action. The chassis, suspension and tires weren't ready for truly rigorous activity off the pavement but did allow the rider to tag along for a while. Carrying a 174.7cc engine in the frame gave the F7 a decent amount of power. The chassis permitted over 10 inches of ground clearance and the saddle height was a respectable 32.4 inches off the tarmac. Weight was listed as 254 pounds which may have disqualified it from heavy duty racing action, but was still adequate for serious fun. Top speed was about 75 miles per hour, once again enough to be entertaining while not enough to cause a lot of grief.

The two-stroke engine consisted of a single, vertical cylinder fed by a 26mm Mikuni carb. The F7 was able to attain 46.9 miles per gallon and with 2.4 gallons of fuel aboard a rider could go more than 100 miles before needing to refuel. When delivered new the F7 came equipped with a head and tail light whereas the example seen here has had the lighting removed as was the speedometer and tach that came stock. The front rim and exhaust have also been modified as has the factory fuel delivery system. What we see now is the rubber tube extending from the top of the engine case that allows installation of a much bigger carb than

With the factory lighting and instruments removed this F7 is equipped for a higher level of competition.

The upswept exhaust, complete with small chrome heat shield, has been slightly modified on this example.

Although the exhaust pipe itself has been modified the heat shield remains intact.

Here you can see the "skunk tube," the modified rubber tube needed to install an oversized carb.

what was supplied new. This arrangement was known as a "skunk tube" and was a common revision for riders of the day.

This long list of appealing features was sold new for the agreeable price of $840 on the east coast, $820 on the west. Obviously the F7 was not going to win any races on or off-road but would supply the rider with hours of enjoyable activity aboard its comfortable saddle. The ergonomic layout made it a comfortable perch for most riders under 5'-10" but was often a bit cramped for taller riders. Changes during its five year product cycle were minimal with mainly cosmetic alterations separating the different years.

Finding a machine to restore won't be an easy task but locating parts is not as difficult. The F7 was designed as a nice, all-around machine and by nature they may not have been pampered or kept in top condition. The low cost of entry when new also played a role - they were ridden hard and put away wet, or worse. Despite the lower cost the F7 delivered plenty of fun for riders of almost any skill set.

Kawasaki F7 Model Highlights

The F7 was easy to start and easy to ride for nearly any rider who tried.

A reasonable cost of $ 840 new made it an easy choice for riders on a budget who also wanted a machine capable of many riding styles.

A generous ground clearance of 10.2 inches allowed the F7 to handle some fairly aggressive terrain as long as the tire's abilities weren't exceeded.

The 175cc engine delivered plenty of power for most rider's needs and was easy to start and operate.

The seating position and handlebars made for a comfortable perch as long as the rider was five-foot-ten or less.

Motorcycle Specifications:
1974 F7 175
Wheelbase: 51.3 inches
Weight: 254 Pounds (dry)
Seat Height: 32.4 inches
Displacement: 174.7cc
Gearbox: 5-Speed *Final Drive:* Chain
Fuel Delivery: 26mm Mikuni carburetor
Fuel Capacity: 2.4 Gallons

Horsepower: N/A
Top Speed: Approx. 75 MPH   MSRP: $840
Production: 1971-1975

Motorcycle Ratings
Available Examples: 1 out of 7
Replacement Parts Availability: 3 out of 7
Ease of Restoration: 3 out of 7
Final Value vs Restoration Costs: 2 out of 7

1974 Kawasaki F9-B

Owner: Gary Lingbeck

By the time 1974 rolled into view, the world of off-road motorcycles had grown larger than anyone could have predicted. A few brands had already faded from view and some were on the verge, but the models from Japan continued to grow at a frantic pace. Each of the four primary makers from the region continued to enhance their offerings in both number, size and features in efforts to grab as much market share as possible.

Of this batch the Kawasaki F9 was first seen as a 1972 model. While not offering any space age technology or never-seen technology it was reviewed as a potent machine equipped with a strong 350cc two-stroke engine and five-speed transmission. Fitted with head and tail lights opened up the number of options when time of day played a role. Though the tires were not aggressive enough to be pure off-road gear they could handle paved and unpaved surfaces with aplomb. If either got too demanding a different machine was probably a better selection. There were a number of different offerings available at any displacement you chose including the 350cc class. They were more potent than the smaller models but also a bit trickier to handle when the conditions got rough and were not as easy to toss around if trouble arose.

The classic Candy Gold paint is a perfect fit for a mid '70s vehicle and the black accent stripe adds a nice bit of contrast.

The setup of the F9 was ideal for a variety of riding demands and could even carry a passenger if required.

The 1974 version of the F was actually known as the F9-B and was the only year it was dressed in the Candy Gold hue with the black accent stripe. Among its immediate peers, Honda and Yamaha both sold a 350cc model capable of street and dirt use. Smaller machines had begun the parade but as people grew accustomed to that level of power, most wanted more and thus the 350 segment was born. Even larger models would be seen but they tended to be far more demanding and better suited to the experienced rider.

The tubular steel chassis was standard fare as was the suspension, gearbox and seating. Without

Popular in most off-road machines, including the F9, was the two-stroke, single-cylinder engine.

The upswept exhaust was found on the left side of the chassis, complete with the perforated heat shield.

reinventing the wheel every year many machines carried nearly the same specs but hoped to draw buyers with added features for comfort an convenience. The F9-B came equipped with full instrumentation which at the time was a speedometer and tach mounted atop the bars. The saddle was well padded and could accommodate a passenger as well. A set of foot pegs for a passenger were included which was becoming a more common trait on the dual-purpose models.

As far as pricing goes, the major competitors from Japan were nearly the same price. Some of the other brands sold for nearly 50% more than the big four from Japan but tended to be more hand built than the assembly line bikes like the Kawi F9.

Locating complete examples today isn't as easy as you might think, but there are plenty of online sources that will assist you in your quest.

Kawasaki F9 Model Highlights

The F9 was designed to be an all-around machine that could be ridden on a variety of surfaces by nearly any rider.

The 350cc engine produced 28 horsepower at 6500 RPM and moved the F9 ahead with plenty of zip.

A set of gauges added to the user-friendly nature of the F9 and helped to keep the rider abreast of his actions.

The MSRP was just over $1000 and made buying the F9 an easier choice than many others in the day.

Able to hold nearly 3 gallons of petrol in the tank allowed the rider to enjoy longer stints in the saddle between refueling.

When fully fueled the F9 weighed only 315 pounds which made it easy to ride on different surfaces.

Motorcycle Specifications:
1974 Kawasaki F9 350
Wheelbase: N/A
Weight: 315 Pounds (dry)
Seat Height: N/A
Displacement: 346cc
Gearbox: 5-Speed   Final Drive: Chain
Fuel Delivery: 30mm Mikuni Carburetor
Fuel Capacity: 2.9 Gallons
Horsepower: 28@6500

Top Speed: N/A
MSRP: $1055
Production: 1972-1975

Motorcycle Ratings:
Available Examples: 2 out of 7
Replacement Part Availability: 3 out of 7
Ease of Restoration: 3 out of 7
Final Value vs Restoration Costs:
  3 out of 7

1974 Kawasaki KX250

Owner: Gary Lingbeck

By the time the 1974 model year became a reality, the market for off-road machines had become a busy place. Honda's Elsinore had already carved out a deep segment of the market for its own and although Kawasaki had offered off-road models in the past, a drastic update was needed to regain a competitive advantage. Using their previous years of experience the KX250 was born and released for 1974 in its debut offering.

The new model from Kawasaki really had to make an impact on the buying public if any gains were to be made and the KX250 did just that. Any shortcomings in previous models had to be eradicated and again the KX250 achieved all of that and more. With a weight of only 214 pounds with half-a-tank of fuel, 34 horsepower at 8000 RPM and a list price of $1150, there was very little to complain about. When compared to other machines in the range, the KX250 was easy to start, adding another measure of positive to the balance sheet. The white, angular graphics accenting the Kawasaki green on the tank drew stares wherever it went and drew buyers to the showrooms for a closer look. Team Green knew the buyers had many options to select from so the new KX had to capture more than their imagination with its brightly colored fuel tank. Nearly a dozen other machines were in the same category for 1974 making the pressure to succeed even greater.

The single-cylinder engine displaced 246cc and sipped fuel through a 34mm Mikuni carb. The five-speed gearbox was a favorable improvement over the earlier for-speed variants and as always a single row chain sent the power to the rear wheel. The 55.8 inch wheelbase was almost luxurious in its dimension and added some stability to the often twitchy behavior of off-road models. 7.7 inches of ground clearance was acceptable but far from the best in its class. The saddle height was a little tall at 32.5 inches too.

Complaints in the magazines were minimal, most concerning the plastic fenders which broke easily, along with foot pegs that weren't spring-loaded though they were stronger than previous versions. All in all the new KX250 was a winner at the dealers and on the tracks around the country.

Minor alterations and upgrades were made over the next couple of years, but the debut model was certainly a success. Pressure from other makers did eventually give Kawasaki inspiration for improvements and they made adjustments as required. The latest version of the initial KX250 was produced through the 1976 model year, Kawasaki took a year off for 1977, and brought the KX 250 back for 1978 as a much better motorcycle. The 250cc class was one of the hottest in the market and would remain

The angular slash of the fuel tank graphics helped draw people to the showrooms and the performance earned points on the track.

By making improvements to every facet of the previous offerings, Kawasaki came up with a sure winner in the '74 KX250

With a displacement of 246cc, and wearing a 34mm Mikuni carb, the KX250 delivered a huge punch for its size.

Bold graphics and the well known Team Green hue proved to be the bait required to draw buyers into the fray.

that way for many years until bigger displacement machines were introduced to the eager, power-hungry buyers.

KX250 Model Highlights

34 horsepower at 8000 RPM was considered one of the best in its day and Kawasaki was earning a reputation for their powerful engines both on and off the road.

The light weight of the KX250 helped make performance seem even better, especially when ridden on its primary home of off-road terrain.

The 246cc engine was easy to start and made buying it an easy choice when compared to some of the stubborn starters seen elsewhere on the market.

The official Kawasaki Lime Green continued to be a popular selection and was recognizable anywhere it went.

Adding another gear to the transmission gave the now 5-speed version greater flexibility when conditions changed rapidly as they so often did on the off-road surfaces.

The wheelbase brought a hint of stability to the game when the KX was forced to travel on sections of smoother surfaces and brought some civility when things got rough.

Motorcycle Specifications:
1974 KX250
Wheelbase: 55.8 inches
Weight: 214 Pounds (1/2 tank of fuel)
Seat Height: 32.5 inches
Displacement: 246cc   **Gearbox:** 5-Speed
Final Drive: Chain
Fuel Delivery: 34mm Mikuni Carburetor
Fuel Capacity: 2.38 Gallons
Horsepower: 34@8000 RPM
Top Speed: N/A   **MSRP:** $1150
Production: 1974-1976

Motorcycle Ratings:
Available Examples: 1 out of 7
Replacement Part Availability: 3 out of 7
Ease of Restoration: 3 out of 7
Final Value vs Restoration Cost: 2 out of 7

1978 Kawasaki KX250

From its gold anodized rims to the alloy fuel tank the reborn KX250 bristled with new features.

Owner: Greg Lingbeck

Kawasaki first introduced their KX250 as a 1974 model. It became a popular choice and was sold through the 1976 model year with only minor changes. Kawasaki did not sell any motocross machines for 1977 because the previous version of the KX250 was shown to be obsolete by competing machines on the market and the cost to create another new model was deemed too expensive. The public outcry turned out to be more than they could have predicted and a revised version was released for 1978.

It's most obvious alteration was the set of gold anodized alloy rims under the green plastic fenders. The new hoops looked great and gave the KX250 a fresh look but other changes needed to be made to keep up with the other machines being sold in the highly competitive market.

Mechanically the '78 edition did carry some revisions that were welcomed with open arms. An increased compression rating of 7.6:1 helped to boost output along with a larger 38mm Mikuni carb. These two alterations raised the horsepower to 40@8000, and that increase helped to keep the returning KX250 near the head of the class. Enhanced Kayaba front forks and rear shocks with remote reservoirs also gave the latest KX a new quality in the ride and handling department. The rear shocks also provided 9 inches of travel, another welcome boost over the previous version.

The frame tubes were now created using chrome-moly tube for added stiffness while staying light. The ignition was fired by a CDI system, and the cylinder walls were electro-fused (a Nikasil-type process) which eliminated the steel sleeve. To reduce weight the new fuel tank was made from aluminum alloy variety, and the improved front suspension was air adjustable for the first time.

As exciting as the returning 1978 KX250 was, the 1979 adaptation would once again reset the bar for performance and handling. It was given a complete redesign that included a new frame, reshaped fuel tank that was more in keeping with contemporary standards, as well as an increase to 11 inches of wheel travel. The rest of the spec sheet was equally amazing and helped return the venerable KX250 to the top of the heap in an ever expanding universe of off-road machines.

Each year of the KX250 saw new upgrades that improved the breed. 1980 saw the first application of Kawasaki's new Uni-trak suspension in the rear. For 1982 the KX250 found a 220mm disc brake on the front wheel and another bump in the output to 42.5@7500 RPM. Each of the improvements helped keep the once mighty KX250 at the leading edge of the competition and at the finish line at tracks across the USA.

The KX250 would be on the scene in one version or another until 2007. After that the machine again was treated to an entirely new design that was no longer based on the original comeback model of 1978 but continued to rack up sales in the dealerships and wins at tracks across the USA and abroad.

The 250cc two-stroke engine now featured an electro-fused cylinder wall instead of a steel sleeve, and a CDI ignition.

To reduce the shriek of the 250cc engine, and eliminate sparks, the KX250 still utilized a small muffler.

The alloy fitting at the bottom of both fork legs was designed to cool the fork oil, note the cooling fins.

1978 Kawasaki KX250 Model Highlights

Gold anodized rims made a great visual addition to the classic KX250 team.

The engine was given cylinder walls that were electro-fused for added performance.

A frame crafted from chrome-moly tubing added strength while reducing weight.

A CDI ignition assured easier starting for the 250cc single.

Both the fuel tank and swing arm were now made from an aluminum alloy to reduce weight.

The front suspension could be adjusted easily using the air system - added for the 1978 release.

The aluminum swingarm was anodized in gold but sadly that finish has faded badly over time on this example.

Additional ride height gave the KX250 a more aggressive stance and allowed it to be ridden over higher berms than previously.

Motorcycle Specifications:
1978 Kawasaki KX250
Wheelbase: 55.7 inches
Weight: 207 Pounds (dry)
Seat Height: N/A
Displacement: 249cc
Gearbox: 5-Speed
Final Drive: Chain
Fuel Delivery: 38mm Mikuni Carburetor
Fuel Capacity: 2.1 Gallons
Horsepower: 40@8000 RPM

Top Speed: N/A
MSRP: N/A
Production: 1978 – 1982

Motorcycle Ratings:
Available Examples: 2 out of 7
Replacement Parts Availability:
  4 out of 7
Ease of Restoration: 3 out of 7
Final Value vs Restoration Costs:
3 out of 7

1974 Kawasaki KX450

The dimensions of Kawasaki's new MX machine were fairly typical, yet when put together they added up into an entirely new class of off-road motorcycle. The stock lime green color of this example has obviously faded due to too much time in the sun.

Owner: Gary Lingbeck

Kawasaki was never shy about the performance of their motorcycles. First there were the 500 and 750 triples, then the legendary KZ 900, introduced for 1973. For the 1974 model year Kawasaki introduced their brand new KX250 to rave reviews and set a new standard for that form of two-wheeled fun. As if that wasn't enough, another off-road monster was also released the same year, the KX450 was an even meaner green machine than the KX250. Of course the 200 extra cc didn't hurt and the fresh model was built to be a dominant force at the track - Kawasaki doesn't like to lose.

Based on the previous MX model, the 1973 F12MX, the new KX450 pumped up every inch of that model to create the KX450. The F12MX was only Kawasaki's second attempt at a true MX machine and made a good platform for the beefier KX450. A 441cc two-stroke fed by a 34mm Mikuni carb delivered 38 ponies at 5500 RPM. All those ponies were fed to the dirt through a five-speed transmission and chain drive to the rear wheel.

Dimensions for the big 450 included a wheelbase of 55.5 inches and ground clearance of 7.7 inches - together they made for a stable platform with enough space under the frame to clear the biggest obstacle. A small two gallon fuel tank was used to provide the KX450 to finish a race but not a lot more.

The selected hue of Lime Green was

Displacing 441cc and producing 38 horsepower at only 5500 RPM was no small feat and was one of the KX450's greatest strengths.

A set of replacement fenders are seen on this example as the originals never lasted long when raced competitively.

applied to the fuel tank while the fenders were ivory in color. The fenders on the example seen here have both been replaced due to damage to the original set. Broken fenders were a common occurrence for anyone riding an MX machine and the units provided by the factory tended to be somewhat fragile. As a result the Preston Petty Company kept a supply of replacement fenders to every MX machine in use.

Being crafted as a true race machine the KX450 sported no instruments. Again due to the true racing intentions the suspension was basic and very functional in its design, executed with coil-over shocks at the rear and a hydraulic fork up front. In 1974, drum brakes were pretty much the rule for MX machines and the 450 from Kawasaki was no exception.

The light and powerful KX450 remained in the Kawasaki catalog until 2008 although each year showed changes to the popular MX machine. Most of the year-to-year changes were either simple changes to the graphics or minor mechanical upgrades.

A quick online search found only a few examples ready for riding or restoration. Parts websites are a different story with more than enough pieces offered to build a new bike from bits.

Kawasaki KX450 Model Highlights

A powerful 441cc, two-stroke engine was the heart of the newest beast from Team Green. The single-cylinder motor produced 38 horsepower at only 5500 RPM - a major improvement over the previous model.

A dry weight of only 215 pounds was very light for a 450cc bike of the period.

Created as a true race machine the KX450 came without any lighting, or instruments, part of the way Kawasaki kept the weight so light.

Motorcycle Specifications:
1974 Kawasaki KX450
Wheelbase: 55.5 in.
Weight: 215 Lbs (dry)
Seat Height: N/A
Displacement: 441cc
Gearbox: 5-Speed
Final Drive: Chain
Fuel Delivery: 34mm Mikuni Carburetor
Fuel Capacity: 2 Gallons

Horsepower: 38@5500 RPM
Top Speed: N/A **MSRP:** $1350
Production: 1974-2008

Motorcycle Ratings:
Available Examples: 2 out of 7
Replacement Parts Availability: 4 out of 7
Ease of Restoration: 3 out of 7
Final Value vs Restoration Costs: 2 out of 7

1969 Maico X4-A 360

Mounted low on the chassis the exhaust caused an occasional problem in dry conditions but was out of the way of the rider's leg.

Owner: Norm Carroll

Maico began its life in Germany in 1926 and their first offerings were powered by small engines of 98 and 123cc. Time saw the company dabble in a variety of engines and displacements and even toiled with automobiles for a period. In the latter portion of the '60s and into the 1970s there was an explosion of activity in organized off-road racing and Maico was eager to join the fray. Of the products they offered, the Super Moto Cross 360 X4-A showed the most promise.

A frame of tubular steel forming a double loop for rigidity, the 360 was equipped with a single-cylinder engine that really delivered. 354cc in size and two-stroke in function the engine produced 40 horsepower at 6500 RPM. When dry the 360 only weighed 220 pounds making it a powerful yet quite light. The gearbox included four-speeds and a drum brake was found on both hubs. The rear hub was constructed from sections of sheet metal to form the conical shape and resulted in enhanced stiffness with lighter weight. A 55 inch wheelbase and 8-1/2 inches of ground clearance meant it could be ridden on almost any surface without issues. Magazine reviews of the day spoke of the high durability of both the 250 and 360 versions. Getting them started appeared to be a sore spot as was the ease with which the 30mm Bing carburetor flooded the engine.

The 360 was not the largest or smallest model in Maico's 1969 lineup which included 125, 250, 400 and 501cc variations. The square barrel design allowed the 360 to have large cooling fins which did a terrific job of keeping the machine cool even under the harshest of riding conditions. Magazine reviewers of the day rated the comfortable saddle a great place to spend the day. The front forks were considered to be one of the strongest on the market but the rims were a bit softer than desired, causing easier bending than other versions.

The fuel tank held two gallons of precious cargo and was seen in four color options. Red, blue, orange or yellow, both fenders came in the same hue as the tank. The rear fender has a semi-rigid "bib" mounted to the top section but no explanation can be found as to its purpose. Adding some strength would make the most sense as the Germans seldom add a feature with no true purpose.

Maico would be seen in the bankruptcy courts in 1983 despite selling a good quantity of machines and scoring several major wins across Europe and the US. The 1969 Super Moto Cross 360 X4-A sold for $1198 while its slightly smaller sibling the 250 sold for $1048 brand new.

The Maico name has been licensed since their bankruptcy and there were a handful of creations bearing the name, but lacking the hard core nature and bulletproof designs of the older bikes. Locating machines and parts for the late '60s models isn't the hardest task in the world, especially when compared to many other machines shown in this book. Restored value won't be a huge number but the result will be a motorcycle capable of taking on any level of riding you care to throw in its way and come out with flying colors.

Weighing only 220 pounds before adding fuel was one of the Maico's strong suits.

The square shape of the Maico engine adds a lot of square footage to the cooling fins, allowing the big 360 to stay cool under pressure.

Holding only 2 gallons of fuel limited the riding time on the Maico but was a safe haven for the contents.

The square head gives the 360 and its smaller 250cc sibling an aggressive look that suited the machine to a T.

Maico 360 X4-A Model Highlights

A sturdy frame that gave the strong 354cc engine a home was one of the best in the industry.

The motor, once started, was tough to stop no matter what conditions were thrown its way.

Despite its rugged design and construction, the 360 weighed only 220 pounds before adding fuel, putting it in the same class as many cycles of smaller displacement.

The saddle was well cushioned and provided the rider with a high level of comfort regardless of the riding conditions.

The front forks were very stout and delivered precise handling when taken off road.

The square barrel design of the engine's cylinder allowed for more cooling fin area which helped to keep the 360 cool.

Available in four colors to match the tank, the heavy duty fenders resisted breakage better than most.

Motorcycle Specifications:
1969 Maico 360 X4-A
Wheelbase: 55 inches
Weight: 220 Pounds
Seat Height: N/A
Displacement: 354cc
Gearbox: 4-speed
Final Drive: Chain
Fuel Delivery: 300 Bing Carburetor
Fuel Capacity: 2 Gallons
Horsepower 40@6500 RPM
Top Speed: N/A
MSRP: $1098
Production: 1968-1969

Motorcycle Ratings:
Available Example: 2 out of 7
Replacement Part Availability:
  4 out of 7
Ease of Restoration: 3 out of 7
Final Value vs Restoration Cost:
  2 out of 7

1973 Monark GS 125

The side view lets us take in the beautiful blue paint on the frame with the sunshine yellow paint in the tank and fenders. This example is beautifully restored but has a few errors in the execution.

Owner: Rod Gorzny

In the world of off-road motorcycles, Monark is not a name that comes to mind immediately unless you have had exposure or experience with the machines they made. A Swedish builder, they completed their first machine in 1920 and sold it under the brand name of Esse. The first batch of cycles bearing the Monark crest came in 1925. As was typical of the period, small displacement, two-stroke engines ruled the roost and the Monark brand did not stray from that path. From 1928 to 1936 the Monark catalog was filled with a variety of models to choose. Any efforts for the civilian market went on hold in 1940 when Monark released their first Swedish military bike in 1942. Once the war ended Monark returned to producing and selling many machines powered by small displacement engines.

First appearing as 1972 model, the GS125 was another model in a sea of existing bikes and brands. It was not imported into the US in its debut year. For 1973 the Monark came to the USA in a limited capacity, with one copy going to each dealer. The only people who could buy it were riders with winning credentials. The 1974 edition could be purchased by anyone with the $1395 it took to ride one home. The GS was sold as an enduro with lights or as an MX, stripped of all pieces that weren't required for MX competition. The Monark product offered the buyer a unique blend of high-quality components along with some quirky features that didn't sit as well with the riders in the USA. Magazine reviewers spoke of the ease of riding the GS125 presented but how the bars were a bit higher than they liked and the steel tank sat up enough to cause some issues during hard braking. The brakes were lauded as terrific while the shocks didn't get any new fans. One tester claimed it would simply go as fast as you dared push it and seldom if ever gave the rider grief for doing so.

As with so many other overseas brands that found success in the states, the arrival of the Japanese makers changed all the rules. Different models, sizes and equipment, all sold at lower prices than the Euro brands could meet or beat, sent them all packing by the early to mid 1970s. The Monark GS125 would only be offered for three years, 1972, 1973 and 1974. This probably goes without saying, but a limited production run results in only a handful of machines and parts that can be found today. There is at least one website dedicated to the vintage Swedish cycle maker, but the bikes remain few and far between.

The Monark logo wore a proud crown and gave credit to its home country, Sweden. If done correctly the tank would be fitted with rubber knee pads.

The 122cc Sachs engine propelled the GS125 smartly due to light weight and ample power. This is the correct engine for the model, but the airbox shroud is missing and the up pipe is from an enduro edition.

The high mounted exhaust and spark arrester are visible on the right side if the GS and the layout is classic off-road cycle.

On duty to keep things quiet and spark free is the muffler/spark arrester at the end of the exhaust pipe.

Chrome plated, the heat shield on the Monark was a bit flashier than others on the market.

Monark GS125 Model Highlights

Magazine reviewers of the day spoke highly of the way the GS125 behaved under pressure and seemed to give confidence to riders with less experience.

The bike's lightweight nature assisted riders of any style - the GS was easy to throw into corners and recover safely.

The components that went into the assembly of the Monark GS125 were mostly regarded as high grade with a few niggling exceptions.

The beautiful blue used to finish the frame contrasted nicely with the bright yellow finish on the fuel tank and fenders.

Considered a tad pricey for its size, the GS was able to redeem itself once underway.

The example pictured here is a 100% correct restoration. It is owned and was restored by Scott Wallenberg whose father was an importer of the Monark brand in the early '70s. Take note of the shocks, hubs and tank pads that are missing or incorrect on our other machine.
Photo courtesy of Scott Wallenberg

Motorcycle Specifications:
Monark GS 125
Wheelbase: 52.5 inches
Weight: 201 Pounds (dry)
Seat Height: 32 inches
Displacement: 122cc
Gearbox: 6-Speed
Final Drive: Chain
Fuel Delivery: 28mm Bing Carburetor
Fuel Capacity: N/A
Horsepower: 24@5700 RPM

Top Speed: N/A
MSRP: $1395 (1974)
Production: 1972-1974

Motorcycle Ratings:
Available Example: 1 out of 7
Availability of Replacement Parts: 1 out of 7
Ease of Restoration: 2 out of 7
Final Value vs Restoration Costs: 4 out of 7

1974 Montesa Cota 123T

As we've seen on other Montesa models the alloy fenders offset the bright red body work nicely even if they were prone to bending.

Owner: Tony Glueck

Montesa first got its feet dirty in the off-road business in the mid-'50s. They opened their doors in 1944 but spent some time designing cycles for street and road race use. The surge in the off-road competition series has roots in Europe and would soon spread to the USA. Most of Montesa's first years serving the off-road riders were focused on the market in Spain and Europe and didn't pay much attention to the overseas activity until it had already turned hot. Once the trials madness reached the shores of the US it was impossible to not notice how popular the sport had become.

With intentions of gaining some business in the expanding trials field Montesa introduced a series of machines aimed for use in that branch of the off-road riding world. The ability to maneuver around and over obstacles without your feet touching the ground was the challenge riders faced in the trials world. Any machine designed to compete needed to be light, powerful and very narrow in order for the rider to pass through tiny spaces between trees and rocks.

The Cota 123T made it's debut as a 1974 model, as seen here. The factory designation was the 28 M but most buyers used the 123T denomination to order their Montesa. Tipping the scales at 156.5

The one-piece body gave the Cota 123T a sleek appearance, as if it was moving while standing still.

The compact 123.7cc two-stroke engine was pinned into the tubular steel frame and delivered good output for its size.

Mounted low on the fork leg, the rider could see the speedometer when standing, which is the default riding position when aboard a trials machine.

pounds before fuel was added meant the Cota 123T was svelte. A short wheelbase of 49.5 inches carried a 123.7cc two-cycle engine in the simple steel tube frame, mated to a six-speed gearbox. A 25mm carb from Amal measured the fuel going in and a blacked-out exhaust sent the fumes packing. Some of the Montesas had a tiny pillion for the rider while the 123T and others featured a fuller sized saddle, although most trials riders never used the seat unless they stopped for a train. The single cylinder engine had natural silver cases with polished covers and a black cylinder. Keeping a trials machine narrow is a key factor and the Cota 123T had its systems tucked-in close so as not to impede progress.

The Cota 123T was built for three years, 1974 through 1976, and racked up some strong production numbers in its brief reign. More versions of the 123T would emerge prior to the absorption of Montesa by Honda, and every model remains a hot collector item with many parts easy to find for your restoration project.

1974 Montesa Cota 123T Model Highlights

The light weight of the Cota 123 combined with a powerful engine made it a great competitor out on the trials circuit.

The sweeping body work was still a real eye-catcher and helped set the Montesa machines apart from the crowd.

The compact layout and short wheelbase gave the Cota 123T a real advantage against some of the other trials cycles.

Able to carry only 1.2 gallons of fuel there was no weight penalty, even when filled to the brim.

The extended saddle was a nice touch but most trials riders only used the seats when at a complete stop for an extended period of time.

The six-speed gearbox provided riders with an extra ratio when compared to many other machines.

Unlike most of the motorcycles in the world the mounting tabs for the control levers were an integral part of the actual bar.

The concise nature of the Cota 123 T's intentions were obvious, especially once on a twisted trials course.

Motorcycle Specifications:
Montesa Cota 123T
Wheelbase: 49.5 inches
Weight: 156.5 Pounds (dry)
Seat Height: 30.3 inches
Displacement: 123.7cc
Gearbox: 6-Speed
Final Drive: Chain
Fuel Delivery: 25mm Amal Carburetor
Fuel Capacity: 1.2 Gallons

Horsepower: N/A
Top Speed: N/A   MSRP: N/A
Production: 1974-1976

Motorcycle Ratings:
Available Examples: 2 out of 7
Replacement Parts Availability: 6 out of 7
Ease of Restoration: 5 out of 7
Final Value vs Restoration Costs:
** 3 out of 7**

1975 Montesa Cota 172

Owner: Gary Lingbeck

Montesa was a Spanish company that set down roots in 1944 with two partners, one of which would leave later to start Bultaco. The initial prototype was built using a French Motobecane model and was fitted with a 93cc motor with no rear suspension.

The gleaming alloy fenders contrast nicely with the glowing red finish of the body work and makes the Montesa a great looking machine.

The big brother to the Cota 25 is the Cota 172, designed for use by full grown adults while remaining a small machine.

A total of 22 of these were sold which gave the new company enough traction to move forward with plans for more. A 125cc model came next and was entered into races of many types to find what events best suited their designs. Victories in several of the events gave the Montesa name credence and permitted them to move even further along with their plans.

For many years, Montesa aimed most of their early models at street use or road racing. It was only in the late '60s when they saw the growing demand for off-road and enduro models both abroad and in the USA that they decided to enter the off-road market. Before long, many of those bikes were bound for the US, in an effort to keep up with demand. Trials events had begun years before in Europe but were gaining exposure and interest in the states. Montesa answered that need by building machines that were simple, narrow and very light, to make it as simple as possible for riders to follow the course filled with all manner of obstacles.

A fairly typical Trials bike from Montesa, the Cota 172 used a 157cc two stroke engine and six-speed transmission to carry the rider up and over tree stumps and rocks.

The skinny, minimalistic frame spaced the axles 49.6 inches apart, and set the seat height at 30.3 inches.

For power, the Cota 172 relied on a 14.5 horse, 157cc two-stroke. Power moved from the engine through a 6-speed transmission and by chain drive to the rear wheel.

A normal pair of coil-over shocks suspend the tail of the bigger Montesa and do a fine job on the 160 pound machine.

Debuted in 1974, a total of 1990 units were built before the Cota 172 was taken out of production a few years later.

Over the years, Montesas earned a reputation for some finicky behavior, but also gained some loyal fans who seemed willing to accept the odd activities as "normal" for a machine of that vintage. A wide range of models were seen prior to the financial woes of the early '80s that forced the company to accept a major buyout from Honda to remain in production.

1975 Montesa Cota 172 Model Highlights

The Cota 172 used reduced dimensions to achieve a great handling trials machine.

Before filling the tank the Cota 172 weighed only 160 pounds The flowing body work was a single unit that did little more than cover the chassis and part of the motor, and hold fuel, and give the rider a small place to rest.

The simplicity of the design, built from a minimum of parts, makes for easy maintenance and repair.

Motorcycle Specifications:
Montesa Cota 172
Wheelbase: 49.6 inches
Weight: 160 Pounds (dry)
Seat Height: 30.0 inches
Displacement: 157.5cc
Gearbox: 6-Speed
Final Drive: Chain
Fuel Delivery: 20mm Amal Concentric Carburetor
Fuel Capacity: 1.2 Gallons

Horsepower: 14.5@7000 RPM
Top Speed: N/A
MSRP: N/A
Production: 1974-1980 1990 Total

Motorcycle Ratings
Available Examples: 1 out of 7
Replacement Parts Availability:
   2 out of 7
Ease of Restoration: 2 out of 7
Final Value vs Restoration Costs:
   3 out of 7

1975 Montesa Cota 25

Looking at the Cota 25 on its own the tiny dimensions aren't as obvious until you get closer and see how truly compact it is.

Owner: Gary Lingbeck

As seen elsewhere in this book the Montesa Cota series was offered in several styles and displacements. The 1975 Cota 25 actually had an engine that claimed 48.7cc using a single cylinder, two-stroke configuration. The sleek molded body was also used on some of the bigger models and still looks great in this down sized format. Fuel capacity was rather small at just over ½ gallon but the great fuel economy it didn't require much to get around. Tipping the scales at 86 pounds didn't hurt the range either.

Designed as a machine for a young child or perhaps as a pit bike, the Cota 25 did not enjoy brisk sales in its 7 year run racking up only 1800 sales. The 50M model was fitted with a manual three-speed gearbox while it could also be purchased with an automatic version in the 10M model of which far more were produced. Neither version sported any lighting, only a square number plate up front was found to place your rider number at races.

The small pillion was a formality since the Cota 25 was aimed at the trials riders who spent 98% of their day standing as they traversed the unusual terrain at really slow speeds. Coil spring shocks at the rear were joined by hydraulic forks up front to provide the rider with a minimum of suspension travel. Stopping was handled by a pair of tiny

Designed as a trials machine, the small pillion gets very little use anyway so its tiny dimensions don't take anything away from the value.

The scaled down dimensions of the Cota 25 did nothing to take away from its great appearance.

drum brakes, one at each wheel. With a terminal velocity of only 24.85 MPH you didn't need much to slow down the Cota 25.

Offered from 1974 through 1982 the manual gearbox model was never intended to be a blockbuster in sales and in that regard wasn't a disappointment to Montesa or anyone else. Its tiny dimensions and power held it to only minor action while looking great. As great as it appears, finding parts for a machine of this production level will be a true challenge, forcing many who desire to own one to look at other machines with bigger production runs.

1975 Montesa Cota 25 Model 50M Model Highlights

The diminutive dimensions and limited power will keep a serious rider from competing, but getting around the pits will be a breeze

Smaller and younger riders will be able to get some valuable experience aboard the Cota 25 as it does offer a stable platform even under full power.

Weighing less than 100 pounds the Cota 25 is easy to haul around between events and on the way to and from such activities.

The automatic variant (Model 10 M) removed another complication from the equation for inexperienced riders and can give them their first taste of two-wheeled fun.

The single cylinder mill delivers 1.57 horsepower at 4500 RPM so getting in trouble from using too much throttle isn't seen as an issue.

Motorcycle Specifications:
1975 Montesa Cota 25 Model 50 M
Wheelbase: 37 inches
Weight: 86 Pounds (dry)
Seat Height: N/A
Displacement: 48.7cc
Gearbox: 3-Speed   Final Drive: Chain
Fuel Delivery: 14mm Dell 'Orto Carburetor   Fuel Capacity: .53 Gallon
Horsepower: 1.57@6500 RPM
Top Speed: 24.85 MPH   MSRP: N/A
Production: 1800 1974-1982

Motorcycle Ratings:
Available Examples: 2 out of 7
Replacement Parts Availability:
  2 out of 7
Ease of Restoration: 2 out of 7
Final Value vs Restoration Costs:
  3 out of 7

1972 OSSA Mick Andrews Replica

The Mick Andrews Replica looks the part of the factory model and shares many of the features that made it a champion.

Owner: Mike Reusch

In the world of off-road motorcycles the term "replica" comes up quite often. It is applied to a street legal or civilian version of a factory racing machine. In this case the OSSA Mick Andrews Replica (MAR) was built to commemorate the back-to-back wins at the Scottish Six Day Trials by a gentleman named Mick Andrews. People who won this event once were considered kings so to win it two years in a row earned Mick true legendary status.

Modeled closely after his factory race machine (he help in creating it), the OSSA MAR you could buy was almost a direct copy of what was ridden to take the top step on the podium with a few exceptions. A period magazine review raved of the performance, handling and build quality and had only a few niggling complaints. At that point in off-road history there were so many machines competing for the consumer's dollar it was scary.

One of the biggest factors in the MAR's success was its light weight. Before adding fuel it didn't even register 200 pounds on the scales. A capacity of only 1.8 gallons of fuel barely nudged it over the 200 mark and light weight in a trials machine is a key ingredient in a successful recipe. Riding a trials bike in an event is a delicate mix of balance and having the proper ratios in the gearbox. The first 3 were crucial for the actual course while the 5th gear is only used for dashing from one point to another where crawling over rocks isn't part of the game. The weight balance on the MAR was 44% at the front with the rest at the rear wheel. The foot pegs position was another critical measure and those fitted to the MAR were exactly where they belonged although they were deemed a bit slippery by the magazine review.

The diminutive machine had a wheelbase of only 52 inches and a seat height of 31 inches off the tarmac. Ground clearance of 10.2 inches was worthy as was the 19 horsepower at 6500 RPM. From every direction it appeared that the "replica" was an almost identical mimic of the actual factory entrant campaigned by its name sake.

A two-stroke, single-cylinder engine displacing 244cc was bolted in the frame and acted like the lower segment of the chassis. A sturdy skid plate was in place to protect the lower regions of the motor from rocks and rugged conditions. The engine was fitted with a single 26mm IRZ Concentric carburetor that also worked well in testing. Small drum brakes were located at both ends and did an admirable job of slowing the tiny MAR from a typically slow and deliberate pace.

The white paint with green accents was another tribute to the machine raced by Mr. Andrews but I bet the $940 price tag was a bit lower than what it took to build and campaign a factory machine, and win, twice. The Mick Andrews Replica was offered through OSSA for 6 years and was last seen as a 1978 edition. Little changed besides graphics but after getting the first effort so right, why mess with success?

OSSA Mick Andres Replica 250 Model Highlights

A tank capable of holding 1.8 gallons didn't add much weight even when full.

Another detail designed to save weight were the openings cut into the clutch cover.

The two-stroke single displaced 244cc and was used as part of the frame.

The small metal cage helped prevent damage to the headlight and was crafted from light weight material.

The side cover detailed the victories of Mick Andrews and the green accent stripe added style.

The diagonal slash on the fuel tank was intended to commemorate the victories aboard the factory racer in 1971 and 1979.

The engine was employed as a stressed-member and replaced the lower section of the frame tubes to save weight.

A durable skid plate was used beneath the engine to protect it from damage caused by rough terrain.

Designed for use as a trials machine, the low weight of the MAR was one of its greatest strengths.

The build quality of the OSSA was one of best on the market.

Highly effective suspension at both ends was joined by a set of tiny drum brakes to slow the machine when required.

Having only a 52 inch wheelbase and a weight of 212 pounds the MAR was truly a tiny yet very sturdy offering from OSSA.

Motorcycle Specifications:
1972 OSSA Mick Andrews Replica 250
Wheelbase: 52 inches
Weight: 212 Pounds (half tank of fuel)
Seat Height: 31 inches
Displacement: 244cc
Gearbox: 5-Speed
Final Drive: Chain
Fuel Delivery: 26mm IRZ Concentric Carburetor
Fuel Capacity: 1.8 Gallons

Horsepower: 19@6500 RPM
Top Speed: N/A   **MSRP:** $940
Production: 1972-1978

Motorcycle Ratings
Available Examples: 2 out of 7
Replacement Part Availability:
   2 out of 7
Ease of Restoration: 2 out of 7
Final Value vs Restoration Costs:
   2 out of 7

1976 OSSA Desert Phantom

The fenders that came as part of the factory package looked great but were easily cracked or broken as reported by magazine reviews of the day.

Owner: Mike Reusch

OSSA's beginnings run back to 1924, the company enjoyed a long and successful run before being overcome by the competition from Japan. Of the motorcycles they sold through the years the Phantom and Desert Phantom were two of the most memorable, and sought after by collectors today.

Differences between the two were minimal but each was designed to tackle a certain type of terrain. It doesn't take a genius to guess what the Desert Phantom was geared towards, and it carried several unique characteristics that gave the Desert version an upper hand in that sandy environment.

Of the subtle differences, the Desert came with slightly different gear rations in it's five-speed transmission. The swingarms were also two different animals. The MX models came with an aluminum unit while the Desert special used a chrome moly swingarm one inch longer than the MX's. The Desert Phantom also didn't come from the factory with a method of attaching lights for after dark use. However, the Motoplat equipment could be added prior to delivery or could be added later at a higher cost. The compression rate on the Phantom was listed at 13.2:1 while the desert animal had a lower ratio of 10.5:1 which better suited the demands of riding through the sand.

The single-cylinder engine in the Desert Phantom came with less compression, and slightly different gear rations, than the MX version.

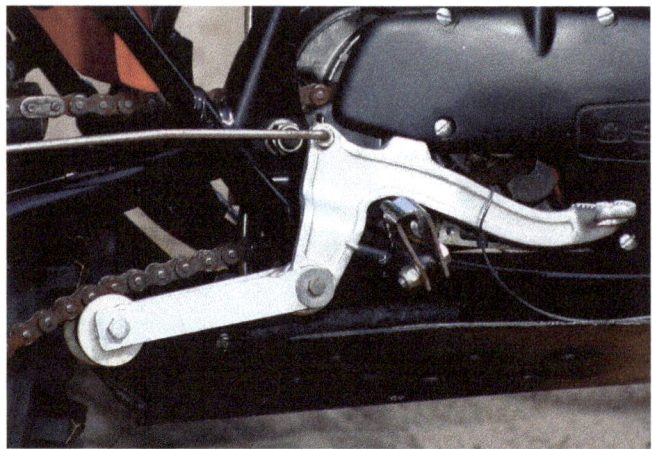
A nice feature on the Desert Phantom was the automatic chain tensioner that kept the correct level of tension on the final drive chain.

Outside of the different compression ratios, each machine was fitted with the same 244.3cc single-cylinder engine mated to a five-speed gearbox. A 36mm Bing carburetor was on duty to dole out the fuel as required and 3 gallons could be stored in the fuel tank. Dry weight was listed as 207 pounds.

Suspension at both ends hailed from Betor and that included front forks with 6.6 inches of travel, while the rear coil-overs delivered 4.2 inches and were adjustable five ways. Together, the forks and shocks gave the Desert bike 7-1/2 inches of ground clearance. Seat height was listed as 34 inches while the foot pegs were 13 inches from the pavement. The time frame that the Phantom and Desert Phantoms were sold (1974-1976) was the same period where the Japanese machines were pouring into the US. After years of being near the top of the heap in the off-road universe, OSSA and several other brands found themselves floundering for sales. For the debut year of the Desert model the MSRP was $1625. A similar machine from Kawasaki sold for $500 less than that - and the variety of machines coming into the country was staggering. Locating a complete OSSA now is rather a challenge as are the required parts to restore one and keep it running.

OSSA 250 Desert Phantom Model Highlights

Unique gear ratios were provided to better suit desert riding.

Weighing only 207 pounds it was an easy machine to maneuver regardless of the terrain.

OSSA had earned a reputation for building high quality machines and the Desert Phantom was no exception.

Motorcycle Specifications:
1974-1976 OSSA Desert Phantom
Wheelbase: 55.25 in.   Weight: 207 Lbs
Seat Height: 34 inches
Displacement: 244.3cc
Gearbox: 5-Speed   Final Drive: Chain
Fuel Delivery: 36mm Bing Carburetor
Fuel Capacity: 3 Gallons
Horsepower: 19@8000 RPM

Top Speed: 76 MPH   MSRP: $1635
Production: 1974-1976

Motorcycle Ratings:
Available Examples: 2 out of 7
Replacement Part Availability: 3 out of 7
Ease of Restoration: 3 out of 7
Final Value vs Restoration Cost:
   3 out of 7

1972 OSSA Pioneer 250

The high-mounted exhaust system and flowing bodywork give the Pioneer the stance of a real workhorse, which it was.

Owner: Mike Reusch

OSSA is a Spanish company that got its start in 1924, but didn't produce motorcycles until 1949. Up until that date they created movie projectors and were not the only company to start in one field and switch to another later on. From the beginning OSSA motorcycles gained a reputation for being fast, dependable and easy to ride whether on the track or off.

The Pioneer had a sibling that was a kissing cousin named the Stiletto. The Pioneer was slightly detuned from the Stiletto specs but retained many of the quality features. The Pioneer 250 first appeared as a 1968 model and continued through the 1973 model year. Powered by a 244cc single-cylinder, two-stroke engine, rated at 21 Horsepower. Though that doesn't sound like a winning number, riders proved that there's more to a successful machine than mere ratings.

Before adding fuel and other fluids the Pioneer weighed about 240 pounds, which was neither the lightest nor the heaviest in its class.

A five-speed gearbox was typical for the period as was the chain drive to the rear wheel. Ground clearance of more than 10 inches was good for nearly any riding terrain but the seat height was a bit tall at 32.5 inches. Power output was rated at

The speedometer assisted enduro riders as they attempted to keep within a range of speed that allowed them the most precise time between check points and also came in handy when riding on the street.

Finished in matt black from stem to stern the exhaust was mounted high to avoid setting brush fires and the heat shield protected the rider's leg from burns.

The plastic used on the later edition Pioneers was extremely flexible which minimized breakage.

21@7800 which was also a bit lower than many others in the 250 class. It was the way the Pioneer worked and rode that defined its status as a rock star, and many magazines in the day claimed the same. A terminal velocity of 72.69 MPH was respectable but no record setter. The single jug was fed through a 29mm IRZ carb and the spent fumes made their way through an expansion chamber before exiting through the high-mounted muffler.

Features on the Pioneer 250 included a speedometer, head and tail lights. This did not make it street legal, you needed a horn for that classification, but at least you could determine how fast or slow you were going, even at night. A three gallon fuel tank meant you could enjoy a bit more time in the saddle than many period machines that stored 2 gallons or less in their tanks. A 21 inch front wheel was mated to an 18 inch hoop at the rear and both were wrapped with knobby off-road rubber. Per the market at the time, 5.5 inch drum brakes were installed at either end.

Production of the Pioneer 250 ended after the 1973 model year and the end of the OSSA company came within a decade of that. A merger with Bultaco in 1979 did nothing to aid the cause and 1982 marked the end for OSSA. Despite the end of the firm in the '80s a great supply of parts can be found with today's online and third party vendors. The dependable nature and ease of riding the Pioneer 250 left its mark on buyers and many seek to own a version of their previous OSSA again today and lucky for them the market is not a complete wasteland in that regard.

1972 Pioneer 250 Model Highlights

The terrific power band of the Pioneer 250 didn't need a five-speed gearbox but the added ratio did add some flexibility to the equation.

Great handling was one of the landmarks of the model with riders of other

The single-cylinder two-stroke engine displaced 244 cc and produced 21 horsepower.

brands considering a change of teams.

The suspension was hailed as a miracle of modern science in the day by at least one large volume magazine.

The Pioneer 250 carried an MSRP of $940 which was a bit higher than many in the day, but not an outrageous figure.

A three gallons tank gave the rider more time in the saddle.

The speedometer and lights at both ends extended the bike's usability.

By reading the specs you would not be impressed, but one hour after climbing aboard the Pioneer 250 you'd be a believer.

Motorcycle Specifications:
1972 OSSA Pioneer 250
Wheelbase: 54 inches
Weight: 240 Pounds (dry)
Seat Height: 32.5 inches
Displacement: 244cc
Gearbox: 5-Speed
Final Drive: Chain
Fuel Delivery: 29mm IRZ Carburetor
Fuel Capacity: 3 Gallons
Horsepower: 21@7800 RPM

Top Speed: 72.69 MPH
MSRP: $940
Production: 1968-1973

Motorcycle Ratings
Available Examples: 2 out of 7
Replacement Parts Availability:
  4 out of 7
Ease of Restoration: 3 out of 7
Final Value vs Restoration Cost:
  3 out of 7

1973 OSSA 250 Six-Day Replica

The latest OSSA sported some great new graphics and promised a world of improvement over the Pioneer it replaced.

Owner: Mike Reusch

The OSSA brand began in Spain in 1924 making movie projectors. They moved into motorcycle production years later and achieved a well-deserved reputation for building diverse and durable machines for use on and off the road.

It has becoming common practice for companies to use the name "replica" when releasing new models to the public. The term suggested the bike you bought to ride is an exact match to the factory race bike of the same period. Sadly marketing doesn't always tell us the whole truth but the OSSA Six-Day replica that was introduced as a 1973 looked the part. Its predecessor, the Pioneer, had gained a loyal following despite a few minor issues. When OSSA released the SDR they had plans to correct those issues and get an even better machine as a result. Both the Pioneer and the new SDR were designed for use as enduro machines, making them capable of on and off-road use. The minor issues for the Pioneer had been not enough top-end power, poor handling at upper speeds and lackluster brakes. OSSA promised that the new SDR would correct all of those issues and deliver an improved machine to offset the added cost.

The OSSA 250 Six-Day Replica made its debut for the 1973 model year and looked terrific in its new white base with red accents. The rear tire was really beefed-up and overall it looked ready to take on any six day event you could throw at it. As it turned out the bigger rear tire caused problems with alignment due to the compact nature of the swingarm. The new SDR weighed two pounds more than the Pioneer it replaced but claimed three more horses at 500 additional RPM. The previous IRZ carb was swapped out for a larger 32mm Amal Concentric unit that helped provide the added power. An extra half-inch was seen in the wheelbase but the seat height remained the same. Fuel capacity and top speed were unchanged and it appears that the biggest alteration in the new SDR besides the colors and graphics was the new price, which was higher. The Pioneer set a rider back $940 while the new model would require $ 1180.

A CYCLE WORLD review done in the August 1973 issue rode the SDR with anticipation of it being a vastly improved model even though the Pioneer was never considered a poor machine. By the end of their extensive testing they deemed the new OSSA 250 Six-Day Replica to be no better at anything and maybe a bit worse. Those results were not exactly what OSSA had planned when redesigning the Pioneer, giving the latest edition a short life span. Due to the nature of that fact, finding examples today will once again pose a real challenge as will locating the required pieces to turn a basket case into a gem.

1973 OSSA Six-Day Replica Model Highlights

With hopes of being an improved version of the previous Pioneer, OSSA changed a variety of items to achieve the Six-Day Replica.

The catchy new graphics and body work caught the attention of buyers.

Part of the new graphics package: the "250 6 days" art that adorned the top of the tank.

The OSSA name plate was emblazoned on the side of the fuel tank and worked well against the bright red accent stripes.

The 244cc engine of the SDR delivered 3 additional horsepower compared to the Pioneer, more power is always a welcome upgrade.

The exhaust was mounted high and fitted with a chrome heat shield which remained a common practice on off-road machines of the period.

The only instrumentation found of the SDR was the circular speedometer/odometer, a handy feature to have when the rider took to the streets.

The meatier rear tire was another feature that immediately drew the eye of interested riders.

A few additional horsepower with no added weight was a pleasant upgrade.

Changing from the IRZ to a bigger Amal carb was another welcome revision that helped make the SDR easier to start.

The sleek body work was dressed in a vivid red on white scheme that was truly appealing. Sadly the overall machine was a bit of a letdown.

Motorcycle Specification:
1973 OSSA Six-Day Replica
Wheelbase: 54.5 inches
Weight: 242 Pounds (1/2 tank of fuel)
Seat Height: 32.5 inches
Displacement: 244cc
Gearbox: 5-Speed
Final Drive: Chain
Fuel Delivery: 32mm Amal Carburetor
Fuel Capacity: 3 Gallons
Horsepower: 24 @8000 RPM

Top Speed: 72 MPH
MSRP: $1180
Production: 1973

Motorcycle Ratings:
Available Examples: 2 out of 7
Availability of Replacement Parts:
  2 out of 7
Ease of Restoration: 2 out of 7
Final Value vs Restoration Costs:
  2 out of 7

OSSA Hybrid Racing

Owner/Builder: Mike Reusch

You can choose any form of motorized racing and you'll find within those ranks, at least one rider who demands more from his machine. Mike Reusch raced OSSA motorcycles at a professional level for years and was well aware of what they were capable of. Although he didn't suffer from a tragic gap between what he had and wanted, he still wondered about upgrading to a machine of his own making.

Using his experience of racing OSSAs for years, as well as his amazing mechanical abilities, Mike was able to create this, "hybrid" although it doesn't blend two types of power like those on today's market. It is a hybrid due to the blending of several years of parts plus several personal upgrades to further improve the product.

Beginning with an OSSA chassis and body work, he opted to build an engine that would far surpass what his current machine could deliver. The machine pictured here could be called a 1971-1976 OSSA because it contains parts from each of those years. Every new component was an official OSSA racing part which really enhanced the performance. Mike hand formed the exhaust and expansion chamber based on his knowledge of how that portion of the system worked. The chain tensioner is a Joe Bolger item and keeps the chain planted where it needs to be to deliver every ounce of the new power to the rear sprocket.

During the time it took for me to photograph this and the other of Mike's OSSAs in this book, I had a chance to hear each one run. The typical high-pitched noise coming from the factory trim models was about what you'd expect from a machine of that

This side doesn't give any clues to the nature of the build, but once it's running anyone within hearing distance can tell there's something afoot.

Any riders who know their OSSAs will notice the unusual nature of the exhaust, mainly due to the fact that it was hand-formed by the owner for optimum performance.

era and displacement. Once he kicked his hybrid to life, a sound of an entirely different nature emitted from the exhaust. It was far more raucous yet still sounded as if no ounce of energy was being wasted. Taking a small spin in the area where we were setup also told me the response to throttle input was far more immediate with no lag or down time. It was obvious even to a new comer to the off-road arena that Mike's years of experience and mechanical know-how were now paying dividends. The sound reminded me of a light switch. It went from "off" to "ON!" in an instant.

I can only assume that riding this machine has got to make his factory models seem kind of tame by comparison. His hybrid looks like it's factory correct but once it's brought to life an entirely different beast emerges. There's no way for me to predict how much time this monster will spend on the track, but I am willing to bet it'll have a hard time passing the scrutiny of the people in charge of ensuring it's within AHRMA guidelines.

Perhaps he's related to Dr. Frankenstein because this high-output OSSA was created using bits and pieces from the factory racing parts bin, all assembled by Mike himself. I'd be expecting crowds with pitch forks at the next race if I were Mike.

Much of Mike's time building the hybrid was spent right here, using a long list of factory racing parts to boost the engine's output.

Motorcycle Specifications:
OSSA Desert Phantom (Factory Trim)
Wheelbase: 55.25 inches
Weight: 207 Pounds (dry)
Seat Height: 34 inches
Displacement: 244.3cc
Gearbox: 5-Speed
Final Drive: Chain

Fuel Delivery: 36mm Bing Carburetor
Fuel Capacity: 3 Gallons
Horsepower: 19@8000 RPM
Top Speed: 76 MPH
MSRP: $ 1635

1970 Penton Berkshire 100 Enduro

Owner: Rod Gorzny

The Penton name is synonymous with all forms of off-road motorcycling and the brand came to be in 1968. John Penton already had a fabled career in the field of off-road racing and decided that he needed to build a better machine for buyers in the USA. There were numerous overseas brands and models being sold here but he desired more from his own country. He approached several existing companies about building a cycle bearing his name and after several turn-downs the KTM company in Austria said "yes". The earliest Penton machines were based on KTM models, upgraded to specs that John felt were required to be taken seriously.

Sachs motors were used in the premier editions of Penton cycles and the model name tell us what size the engine is. The Berkshire name tells us it's a 100cc version. 125cc models are Six-Day, 175's Jack Pine, 250cc Hare Scrambler and 400cc were known as Mint. Each of the names was borrowed from a famous race or circuit that held the events and his system remains in place today.

This 1970 Berkshire is done in the enduro style, complete with lighting and a simple speedometer. There was also an MX variant that was not equipped with any lights or gauges. From their introduction in 1968 to the 1972 model year, Pentons wore steel fuel tanks as seen here. These models are often called "steel tank…" for obvious reasons. Lighter weight plastic versions were implemented for the 1972 and later models. Penton's desire to create motorcycles that were better than what he'd seen prior resulted in a higher degree of quality in the selected, third-party components and materials.

The left side of the Berkshire shows us the circular air cleaner housing and the compact unitized engine and 6-speed transmission.

The high mounted exhaust is visible on this side, the head and tail lights tell us this is an enduro model.

Penton used the 98cc Sachs engine that KTM had chosen on his early models.

The enduro version of the Berkshire cam equipped with a speedometer whereas the MX models did not.

Ceriani front forks were certainly a step-up from the norm as was the use of chrome-moly tubing for the chassis.

Riders of the Penton brand were usually pleased with the results and were more willing to pay the added cost that most Pentons demanded. Some could be as much as 50% more than a competing model but John Penton refused to compromise on quality to reduce his prices. The Sachs engine that KTM was already using would suffice until he came up with one of his own later on in history. From the beginning John Penton did his best to provide the buyer with the best combination of gear and hardware he thought possible. He would later design and sell a line of accessories that gave riders a few other choices to custom tailor their Penton to suit their tastes.

1971 Penton Berkshire 100 Model Highlights

Using his years of winning on ISDT and MX courses John Penton delivered a new breed of machine that excelled at every facet of the sport.

The blending of upgraded hardware and his own experience at the track produced a line of cycles that really did outperform the rivals.

The MSRP of a Penton was typically higher than some of the competition but that added cost was justified in John's eyes by the high degree of quality he delivered.

Penton used the names of famous tracks and events to allow the buyer a way to easily choose a displacement that suited him best.

The early steel tank versions like the one seen here were later fitted with plastic units to save weight.

Selling machines that performed better than the competition and were easy to ride were two of John Penton's intentions from the start.

Motorcycle Specifications:
1970 Penton Berkshire 100
Wheelbase: 55 inches   Weight: N/A
Seat Height: N/A   Displacement: 98cc
Gearbox: 6-Speed   Final Drive: Chain
Fuel Delivery: N/A   Fuel Capacity: N/A
Horsepower: 16@ XXXX RPM
Top Speed: N/A   MSRP: $635

Motorcycle Ratings
Available Examples: 2 out of 7
Availability of Replacement Parts:
3 out of 7
Ease of Restoration: 3 out of 7
Final Value vs Restoration Costs:
2 out of 7

1974 Penton Berkshire 100 / Vintage Competition MX

Owner/Restorer: Dennis Jones

Within the pages of this book we have seen a variety of off-road machines. Some are restored to former glory, a few are "used," and others, like this one, have been restored, ridden and then converted to a vintage competition machine. The rules tell the owner what alterations can be made, and the owner of this Berkshire Penton did all that was permitted to gain an edge over his competitors. Pentons, by creation, were ready to mix it up with any other cycle at an event but riders always tried new methods of finding a few extra horses or ways to save weight.

This example has seen the benefits of several aftermarket product lines and all that each has to offer. There is still a vast array of products on the market today that allows an owner to upgrade his Penton or to simply return it to its original factory trim. In this case the owner did both, but in stages. He first restored the Berkshire to perfect condition then chose to take it racing which required several alterations to reach the pinnacle of performance.

Typically the first steps in prepping a motorcycle for racing use is to save every ounce possible so that the factory horsepower has less bulk to push around the track. On this Penton Excel alloy rims save a great deal of weight which not only saves bulk but allows the machine to handle better by eliminating unsprung weight. To further enhance handling the factory shocks were replaced with a pair from Works Performance, a company that has a strong record of delivering improved suspension to competitive cycles around the globe. A set of replacement

Although this Penton has been given extensive upgrades to enhance performance it remains true to the classic design.

Revised fenders, rims and rear shocks don't alter the appearance too much, but really boost the performance of this vintage race machine.

The new exhaust boosts power and the lower mounting position keeps it out of the way.

The 98cc Penton engine remains stock internally per the rules of AHRMA.

The Excel alloy rims save weight and the Works Performance shocks bring a new level of control to the Berkshire.

fenders simply keeps things legal without sacrificing original Penton hardware.

Engine performance was enhanced by adding a custom air box to improve breathing. The high pipe was acquired via E.C. Brit's catalog, in addition to further improving breathing, the pipe eliminates weight and relocates the exhaust to a better location on the chassis.

With all of these upgrades, Dennis now enjoys a more powerful Berkshire that handles better than any others he's owned, and he's owned more than a few in his past. He enjoys taking the revised Penton to tracks and often brings home another trophy for the collection. Other times the competitors may best him but he still enjoys a motorcycle that handles better and delivers more smiles than a factory original.

Anyone with a desire to make the same alterations can do so without a lot of effort and some basic mechanical skills. Having restored a long list of Pentons, Dennis' experience makes him an expert in the field.

Motorcycle Specifications:
1974 Penton Berkshire 100
  (Stock Trim)
Wheelbase: 55"
Weight: N/A
Seat Height: N/A
Displacement: 98cc
Gearbox: 6-Speed
Final Drive: Chain
Fuel Delivery: N/A
Fuel Capacity: N/A
Horsepower: 16@XXXX RPM
Top Speed: N/A
MSRP: $635

1975 Penton Jack Pine 175

With a portion of the upswept exhaust covered by the side panel, the view from this side is cleaner than many others whose exhaust is entirely exposed.

Owner: Rod Gorzny

The Jack Pine enduro is a race that was first run it the early part of the 1900s and remains an active event today. Measuring 500 miles and covering a wide array of challenging situations and terrain it is not a ride for the faint of heart. One name that is synonymous with the event is Oscar Lenz. He rode his first Jack Pine aboard a 1912 belt-driven Harley. He went on to ride in the first 14 annual events, winning half of them!

Modern machines taking part in the race today have come a long way since the old belt-drive days but the event remains one of the more grueling you can find. In terms of Penton motorcycles, every Jack Pine model is fitted with a 175cc engine and can often be found competing in the event today.

As we have seen on other Pentons the Jack Pine is always 175cc but can be bought in MX or enduro equipment. As usual the MX variation carries no lighting or extraneous hardware. The enduro version has a tail and head light as well as a speedometer and often times a front fender that hugs the tire in contrast to the MX mounting that rides high on the forks. By this time in Penton history the earlier steel tanks had been replaced with modern molded plastic units that are durable and a lot harder to damage than the metal versions.

Dimensionally the Jack Pine mimics the

Badged a KTM, the engine still wears the radial-finned cylinder head seen on earlier Sachs motors - a design that works so well.

The Girling shocks are complete with piggyback reservoirs and are laid down at an extreme angle for longer suspension travel.

Early versions of the Penton motorcycles all wore steel fuel tanks, which were supplanted with molded plastic units to save weight and reduce damage under rugged riding conditions.

Six-Day models with a larger engine in the frame. Early examples used a Sachs engine while newer variants use a KTM motor. Penton and KTM would continue their partnership until 1978 when KTM bought out Penton. The rear suspension is more radical with the highly angled lay-down shocks for additional suspension travel at the rear. The use of high-grade components was still a mainstay of the Penton brand and Ceriani forks were still used up front with Girling shocks at the rear. The rear shocks seen here are complete with remote reservoirs that allow the units to carry added fluid for reduced fading under harsh use, and better control. The KTM engine displaced 171cc and delivered 26 horsepower to the 6-speed gearbox. The MX models had a 1.8 gallon fuel tank, the enduro slightly larger at 2.4.

Although nearly 40 years old the Penton Jack Pine models can be seen strafing modern day events that are sanctioned by AHRMA as well as smaller events around the country. Availability of Penton chassis is not the toughest search you can take on, but they aren't falling off the trees either. The fact that they were built so well in the day allows them to lead a long life despite the harsh conditions they face on almost every ride.

1975 Penton Jack Pine 175
Model Highlights

Because they were built to very high standards, they can generally be located more easier than some other machines from the same time in history.

The plastic fuel tanks added a lot of resilience to the overall build and took nothing away from the function.

The enduro version allows the rider to take his Jack Pine to ride in more locations and situations, while the MX is a down and dirty race machine.

Parts for the vintage Pentons can still be found as many riders still campaign their antique Jack Piners in events today, a tribute to John Penton and the durability of his creations.

High quality assembly completed using high-grade components can keep a Penton in action for decades after it's retired.

Protruding from its hiding place behind the side cover, the Jack Pine exhaust and muffler do a great job of keeping things quiet, a Penton trademark.

The Penton Jack Pine 175 MX is one the favorite machines ridden by modern day players in vintage events.

Motorcycle Specifications:
1975 Penton Jack Pine 175 MX
Wheelbase: 55 inches
Weight: 226 Pounds (dry)
Seat Height: N/A
Displacement: 171cc
Gearbox: 6-Speed
Final Drive: Chain
Fuel Delivery: Carburetor
Fuel Capacity: 1.8 Gallons (MX)
Horsepower: 26@XXXX RPM

Top Speed: N/A
MSRP: 1245 (MX)

Motorcycle Ratings
Available Examples: 3 out of 7
Availability of Replacement Parts:
  3 out of 7
Ease of Restoration: 3 out of 7
Final Value vs Restoration Costs:
  4 out of 7

1973 Penton Jack Pine 175

The Hi-Point alloy tank is a Penton accessory and adds a little more excitement to a great motorcycle.

Owner/Restorer: Dennis Jones

Within the covers of this book we have seen a variety of off-road motorcycles, most of which have been restored to brand new condition. There are others, like this Penton, that have been modified to participate in vintage racing on tracks around the USA. The owner of this Jack Pine not only takes part in vintage races with his example, but restored it to its current state. As we know all 175cc Pentons are Jack Pine models, named after the Jack Pine Enduro which began in the 1920s.

When upgrading a stock cycle to go racing there are several segments of the machine you can alter and remain within the rules. The alterations to any Penton motorcycle are seldom needed because they such a competent machine to begin with, but yet there some revisions that add to that equation. The OEM shocks were pretty good for the period, but suspension and shocks in general have improved drastically since the early '70s. The Works Performance brand can be found on many off-road models as they enhance ride quality and permit ways to customize the settings to best suit the track and rider.

The fuel tank on this Jack Pine has also been swapped for an alloy model from Hi-

Point. The Hi-Point brand is actually a line of products that were originally sold through Penton dealers as Penton accessory. The Hi-Point catalog offered Penton riders numerous performance related parts that were designed for use on Penton cycles thus assuring a perfect fit. The new fuel tank is retained by a wide leather strap that permits some movement and also provides an easy swap if damage occurs. The alloy knuckle savers are also additional bits that help to protect the rider's hands from low branches that are impossible to ride around.

The remaining assembly and components are as they came from the Penton factory in 1973, and the way they function requires no further upgrade. The bigger engine found in the Jack Pine really boosted the output and placed riders in a different class of racing based on the displacement of the engine.

The level of enhancements seen here do nothing to reduce value if sold in that condition and obviously suit the rider who wants to gain a competitive edge when riding against other riders on motorcycles of other brands and ages. All the revisions are bolt-on allowing for an easy swap back to 100% stock condition if desired. The list of other performance parts can be lengthy but to stay within AHRMA rules one must take care when selecting and installing upgrades.

1973 Penton Jack Pine 175 Model Highlights

The performance of the Jack Pine is in no way diminished by the upgrades - all of which are very available and designed to make a great motorcycle even better.

The Jack Pine as built by Penton and sold by a dealer, came with a set of options so the buyer could customize the bike to his own preferences.

One of the many parts in the John Penton catalog was this alloy fuel tank that mounted directly to the Jack Pine frame.

The exhaust runs hidden behind the side cover and the muffler extends away to keep the fumes from coming back into the rider's face.

The front hub hides only a small drum brake.

As delivered the Jack Pine came with a comfortable saddle that worked well on and off-road.

Locating stock and upgrade parts for the Penton cycles is not all that challenging, and there are loads of support groups - eager Penton owners and riders willing to help.

While Pentons required more cash to buy when new the components used to assemble them certainly justified the added expense.

The radial fins of the Sachs 171cc engine are a trademark item and also do a great job of cooling the aggressive engine.

The Jack Pine is one the best-selling Pentons, not hard to believe given the amazing looks and terrific performance.

Motorcycle Specifications:
1973 Penton Jack Pine 175
Wheelbase: 55 inches
Weight: 226 Pounds (dry)
Seat Height: N/A
Displacement: 171cc
Gearbox: 6-Speed
Final Drive: Chain
Fuel Delivery: Carburetor
Fuel Capacity: 1.8 Gallons (OEM MX)
Horsepower: 26@XXXX

Top Speed: N/A
MSRP: $1245 (MX)

Motorcycle Ratings
Available Examples: 3 out of 7
Availability of Replacement parts:
 3 out of 7
Ease of Restoration: 3 out of 7
Final Value vs Restoration Costs:
4 out of 7

1971 Penton Six-Day 125

The gently curved fuel tank with the concave recesses, and circular air cleaner housing, help to define the classic profile of the Penton Six-Day.

Owner: Rod Gorzny

The Penton tale is often told and the machines wearing his name remain classics in today's world, even decades of their first appearance in 1968. In the first year of sale for the Penton 100cc model, also known as the Berkshire, 400 copies were sold in the US and the company was off to the races, literally. John Penton rode one of the first from that small batch and put the remaining examples into the hands of winning riders. Once their performance was witnessed by the public sales took off.

The Six-Day models were all powered by a 123cc engine, part of John Penton's plan to have each displacement-model wear the name of a famous race or circuit. The ISDT or International Six-Day Trials events were one of the most grueling and put both the rider and machines to tremendous strain. Those that survived were lauded as true winners and crossing the finish line first made you a super hero.

For the Six-Day model, the KTM platform was used, upgraded with Ceriani forks, Girling shocks, Bosch ignition and Bing carburetors - a certain recipe for success. The early examples of the Six-Day and Berkshire models wore the steel fuel tanks as seen here. Later the tanks were upgraded or changed to plastic units that were lighter and easier to produce on a mass

Early models with the sculpted steel tanks received more attention then and now, and require more cash to purchase today.

The Six-Day logo was prominent on the front of the tank and as we know the Six-Day models all sported 123cc engines in the frame.

The Penton kept things light and simple by using an exhaust with an integral heat shield.

scale. With sales of the Penton machines expanding rapidly they needed to alter certain aspects to keep up with demand.

The Six-Day was also treated to a 6-speed gearbox and weighed a scant 198 pounds according to period literature. It could also be purchased in enduro or MX trim depending on your riding plans. The enduro was equipped with lights and a speedometer while the MX edition had no lights or unneeded trim to save weight. The steel tank models are not as easy to locate today due to their more limited production and being made of steel they'd rust away to nothing if not cared for. Finding parts for the remaining craft is not as difficult as some others but will demand some attention to detail to avoid mis-matching model year components. Of course you are free to restore your Penton to any level of accuracy you desire but a purist will retain all of the proper bits for that particular year. Support from Penton owners' groups is one of the strongest found today. They remain very loyal to the creator, John Penton.

Penton Six-Day 125 Model Highlights

As mentioned, each Penton was built to a very high level of quality. Each individual component, and the overall machine, was finished to a level that set Pentons apart from the crowd then and now.

That higher lever of quality throughout meant new Pentons demanded additional cash to buy, compared to most competing brands.

Having KTM agree to assist him in bringing his brand to life was a great decision as they were already building some terrific machines sold under their own label.

The Sachs engine used in the Pentons was a durable and powerful powerplant that served KTM and Penton very well.

The steel tank models command more respect and dollar value today based on the scarcity of remaining examples in pristine condition.

As with other Pentons, and other brands as well, a particular model could generally be purchased as an enduro model with lights and speedo, or a bare-bones MX bike.

The Sachs 123cc engines wore the radial fin design that was also easy to recognize and is rather common in machines of the period.

The same classic view but from this side we find the upswept exhaust finished in matte black.

Motorcycle Specifications:
1971 Penton Six-Day 125
Wheelbase: 55 inches
Weight: 198 Pounds (dry)
Seat Height: N/A
Displacement: 123cc
Gearbox: 6-Speed
Final Drive: Chain
Fuel Delivery: Bing Carburetor
Fuel Capacity: 1.8 Gallons
Horsepower: 21@XXX RPM

Top Speed: N/A
MSRP: N/A

Motorcycle Ratings
Available Examples: 3 out of 7
Availability of Replacement Parts:
  3 out of 7
Ease of Restoration: 3 out of 7
Final Value vs Restoration Costs:
  5 out of 7

Interview with John Young

Factory BSA Enduro Rider 1966-1970

John Young has been active in the motorcycle world for longer than most can recall. He started riding against his father's wishes, but discovered he was a skilled rider. One who continued to improve until BSA picked him up and sponsored him to the number one spot of their two official riders for several seasons.

His mechanical skills are also legendary, which plays well into his continued love for old motorcycles.

John continues to own, restore and collect unusual motorcycles and four of his machines are featured in this book. His business of restoring old and unusual cars keeps him busy, but he still rides on the street from time to time. He rode against John Penton for a while but due to some scoring discrepancies at a major event their friendship remained "like an ex-wife and husband" for awhile.

In addition to his wins for BSA, John rode nearly all the popular brands, including Can-Am, OSSA, MX and American Eagle. photo: Walden Wright

DM: John, how old were you when you first knew you wanted to ride a cycle?

John: My father didn't like motorcycles and forbid me to own or ride one. When I was five years old I helped him at his gas station, pumping gas for customers. I got my first scooter when I was six and rode it in an empty lot across from his gas station. When a customer drove in for gas I'd hop off the scooter and help them. My father said I could get a motorcycle when I was 21 based on his idea of me having enough sense to not choose that option at that age.

DM: So when did your first motorcycle come into the picture.

John: I got married to my first wife when I was 18 and she was another one who didn't like cycles, nor did her father and family. A family friend found a motorcycle in baskets and sold it to me for $15. It was a 1951 NSU 251 and once I got it put together I began riding against everyone's wishes. My buddy had an Indian Chief and was riding on cow trails outside of town and I began riding with him and another pal of ours on a Harley chopper.

DM: So you kept riding and things progressed to the next level?

John: After we'd been riding everywhere around where we lived we saw an ad for a 125 mile enduro event and decided we were good enough to enter. Only 13 riders entered and of those only 5 finished and my buddy and I were two of them. He got second and I took home third place. Once we got home my wife saw the trophy, knew I'd been racing and didn't speak to me for a week.

DM: When did your next machine come along?

John: I had been riding a 500cc Triumph twin and even rode in a 500 mile Jack Pine enduro in Michigan and finished the event, a thing many riders failed to do. I was riding an event every Sunday with only a few exceptions and began to think I was getting good enough to ride with the A list guys.

By the end of 1965 the Triumph was worn out and the single cylinder models were gaining in popularity. There was a new BSA 441 on the cover of CYCLE WORLD magazine and I knew that was my next ride. I also discovered the fact that I needed glasses to see clearly and with the combination of better vision and a lighter cycle I became far more able to win races. In the space of one year I won half of all the races I entered at the National Champion level, and after my first two National wins in 1966 BSA approached me to become their factory enduro rider. I also came in contact with a dealer in Hobart, Indiana named John Goodpaster and he provided me with a ton of support and even introduced me to a BSA distributor in New Jersey. We are still in touch and speak often but he was a real boost to my career in the day.

DM: So how long did you ride for BSA?
John: It began in 1966 and went all the way until 1970. At that point the British cycle industry was being crippled by the incoming Japanese machines. BSA gave me a new bike in '67, but couldn't understand why I needed a new one every year. I explained that unlike road racers who tweaked their bikes to meet their own needs and didn't want new machines, I was riding 7000 to 8000 miles a year in the dirt and the bikes got really beaten up.

DM: Any other machines draw your attention at the time?
John: A local dealer gave me a 1968 Yamaha DT-1 to ride, but it was an abysmal machine with all sorts of problems.

DM: Funny to hear that now because they sold a ton of that model in '68.
John: Well it did present itself as being a great all around option but in truth it needed help.

DM: So after the factory ride ended in 1970 did you continue to ride in competition?

John: Oh yeah, I rode until 1979 when a badly broken ankle put an end to my career. Between the BSA era and 1979 I rode MZ, OSSA, Can-Am and even American Eagle for a while. I was the first rider ever to win a national event on the American Eagle. The MZ at the time was a communist built machine which caused me some grief but it was a pretty good machine.

Top: John's riding skills got him a BSA factory ride, and his picture on the cover of this 1967 issue of American Motorcycling.

Left: This official BSA dealer banner also listed John Young and featured an image of him aboard a race-prepped BSA.

1973 Penton Trials 125

Sadly, despite its great looks the Penton 125 Trials has gone down in history as one of the few designs from Penton that didn't fare well in competition.

Owned and Restored by: Dennis Jones

In the grand scheme of motorcycling history, John Penton's participation in the building and selling of machines bearing his name is brief. Although it wasn't a long run, during the years of operation he created some of today's most memorable and collectible models. Many are still used in AHRMA race events and continue to claim top spots on the winner's podium. Of course in nearly every endeavor, think Ford's Edsel, a company of almost any size can release a model to the buying public that doesn't fair as well as the rest. In the Penton history his 1973 Trials 125 was the one that got away.

Often referred to as the Wassel model due to the small fuel tank that came from the company of the same name, the 125 trials model didn't receive glowing magazine reviews and was even panned by some. On paper the machine should have been a hit and by the looks of it Penton had an instant winner. Sadly neither specs on paper nor how it looked could make any difference to how it actually performed. Wassel was a company that began selling parts to those who rode off-road cycles and grew into manufacturing some of their own machines. It was based in England and John Penton met with the owner many years prior and was a good customer of his, adding various components to the Penton models, the 125 Trials included.

As the record books tell us, by 1973 the Japanese builders were not only making inroads but began to dominate the market with their highly competitive machines and wholesale pricing. Based on the performance of the new Penton model, selling them to dealers was a challenge. After the magazine reviews buyers turned away in vast numbers to view and buy better performing machines at a lower cost. Actual production numbers for the 125 Trials model is not known but somewhere around 1000 seems to be the most likely figure. Any machine built with low production numbers will later become a rare beast and this example is no different.

The bike shown here was bought and sold more than once by the current owner and was lovingly restored by his own hands as well. Selling it to a buddy years ago, he hated to see it go but at that point in life it made the most sense. When his buddy decided to sell it he contacted Dennis and it once again returned to his garage for the return to factory specs. It has been ridden in a few AHRMA events but is not as easy as some others to manage and has become a static display piece now, even though it can be fired up and ridden at a moment's notice.

Finding another copy of this iconic machine today will pose one the biggest challenges you can face. With only 1000 built and being sent to dealers in nearly every state of the country, there may still be some out there, but finding it won't be easy. The compact design and attractive components should have resulted in a blockbuster for Penton, but as we know that doesn't always play out as was originally hoped for.

This spring loaded chain tensioner unit helped to keep the chain on the sprockets where it belonged.

The 123cc Sachs engine delivered adequate power and was delivered with two carbs allowing you to install the one that best suited your needs.

Tucked-in close to the frame, the muffler is mounted at an odd angle but suited the narrow configuration of a trials model.

1973 Penton 125 Trials Model Highlights

As with every Penton only the highest grade components were used to build the 125 Trials model.

The beautiful Wassel fuel tank holds only 1.5 gallons of fuel but for action in the Trials arena that was enough for several events.

Wassel was a company that sold parts to individuals and businesses that wanted to upgrade their current machine.

The 123cc engine hailed from Sachs came with a two carburetors, each one meant for a different set of riding conditions.

Intended as a Trials bike, the Penton has 12-1/2 inch of ground clearance and weighs 190 pounds before adding fuel.

A 6-speed gearbox gives a trials rider plenty of options to match the changing conditions of a trials course.

An automatic chain oiler was a unique feature and extremely rare to see intact today.

Alloy fenders matched the fuel tank and made for an appealing appearance but did nothing to aid in the performance of the Penton.

Judging only by the way the 125 Trials model looks, it should earn top ratings.

The graceful lines of the tiny 1.5 gallon Wassel fuel tank adds to the visual appeal and provided plenty of range for a trials machine.

Motorcycle Specifications:
1973 Penton 125 Trials
Wheelbase: 51.5 inches
Weight: 190 Pounds (dry)
Seat Height: 30 inches
Displacement: 123cc   Gearbox: 6-Speed
Final Drive: Chain
Fuel Delivery: 22mm Amal or 27.5mm Bing Carburetor
Fuel Capacity: 1.5 Gallons

Horsepower: N/A
Top Speed: N/A   MSRP: N/A

Motorcycle Ratings
Available Examples: 1 out of 7
Availability of Replacement Parts: 2 out of 7
Ease of Restoration: 2 out of 7
Final Value vs Restoration Costs: 5 out of 7

1974 Rickman/Kawasaki

Regardless of which side you view the Rickman chassis and Kawasaki engine cut a classic profile.

Owner: Gary Lingbeck

The Rickman brothers, Don and Derek, created the Rickman chassis for motorcycle use in 1960 with the intention of producing great looking machines that also worked well. You could buy a Rickman chassis to fit many different engines, and their first editions were aimed at the British brands like Triumph, BSA and Matchless. Once the 1970s arrived they expanded their horizons to include some Japanese classics like the Honda CB750 and Kawasaki Z1 900. The first designs were marketed for use as scramblers, followed by road race versions and then street going models brought up the tail end of their efforts. 1975 was to be their final year of production and the desirability of their chassis are still well documented today.

The motorcycle seen here is a 1974 Rickman motocross chassis fitted with an early Kawasaki F-21M engine, a rarity unto itself. The owner is to credit for the combination and the resulting machine works as well as it looks.

Specifications on the chassis were fairly typical of the period with enhanced quality the key factor in choosing a Rickman frame. this particular frame came with a 55 inch wheelbase, 8-1/4 inches of ground clearance and a seat height of 32 inches. The specs and the

About the only thing that can be considered to be "normal" is the high-mounted exhaust finished in black and wearing a chrome heat shield.

One of the traits of a Rickman chassis was this well rounded tail section that also did duty as the rear fender.

The Kawasaki F-21M engine is a single-cylinder, two-stroke affair of 238cc that delivers ample power for a machine like this weighing just over 200 pounds.

resulting machine worked well enough to be used in a variety of racing formats. Spanish Betor forks up front and Girling shocks at the rear, were both the finest of their day - and typical of the third-party hardware used on a Rickman. The two gallon fuel tank was and integral part of the Rickman package.

The decision to install a rare Kawasaki engine may be controversial but suits the owner fine considering it was his motor to begin with. Used for only a few years in Kawasaki factory models, the F-21M two-stroke engine displaces 238cc and is fed by a 26mm Mikuni carb. In stock trim the motor developed 30 horsepower at 7000 RPM and gave the original machine, as well as the Rickman, plenty of giddy-up. A four-speed gearbox, essentially part of the engine case, came along with the engine.

When dry the Rickman/Kawasaki package weighs in at a light 214 pounds which helps to bring some added zest to the creation. The Kawasaki that donated its motor was built from 1968 to 1970 and was one of the designs that helped to create the off-road craze in the US.

The Rickmans ceased production of their high-end products in 1975 and finding copies now is a challenge even for the savviest hunter. Using a rare Kawasaki mill for this build only adds to the mystique of this home-built special. Locating a Rickman chassis today is going to be easier than locating a Kawasaki engine of this vintage so obviously taking on a project of this nature requires a high degree of passion with an well funded check book.

1974 Rickman/Kawasaki Hybrid Highlights

The scarcity of the main components used to create this cycle bring a new level of excitement to the rider and especially the owner.

Rickman chassis were built to high standards of quality, and the resulting race machines were generally successful on the track or trail.

The Kawasaki engine was a new breed in its day and brought the performance level in the off-road world to a new high.

Without any lights, this one is obviously meant for MX use, and will never be legal for street use.

The front hub, and tiny drum brake are held between the legs of the Spanish Betor fork legs.

With the exhaust mounted on the opposite side this view gives us an uncluttered look at the Rickman/Kawasaki hybrid.

Motorcycle Specifications
Wheelbase: 55 inches
Weight: 214 Lbs (dry)
Seat Height: 32 inches
Displacement: 238cc
Gearbox: 4-Speed   Final Drive: Chain
Fuel Delivery: 26mm Mikuni Carburetor
Fuel Capacity: 2 Gallons
Horsepower: 30@7000 RPM
Top Speed: N/A

MSRP: N/A
Production: N/A

Motorcycle Ratings
Due to the hand built nature of this machine the standard ratings do not apply. It is however a well done combination of rare components that looks great and runs even better.

1976 Rokon RT340 Automatic

Despite its unusual characteristics the RT340 appeared at first to be the same as many other machines on the market at the time.

Owner: Rex Cusumano

It may be true that the Rokon name doesn't come to mind as easily as Honda or Husqvarna when discussing motorcycles, but the company had a fairly long run. It began in the late '50s when a guy named Charlie Fehn decided to create a motorcycle that sent power to both its wheels. His design and experiments created the Trail-Breaker. Sales were OK but he preferred creating versus selling so he sold the entire business to Orla Larsen in 1963. He continued selling the balloon tire model but saw an opportunity in the competition off-road arena.

After several trials and errors a combination of hardware was joined to become the Rokon RT340 in 1973. Powered by a 335cc single-cylinder, the two-stroke engine was mated to a torque converter. The torque converter meant the RT340 was an automatic transmission model, the first of its kind in the motorcycle world. Scooters used them earlier but never before on an actual motorcycle. Much like its oddball predecessor, the RT340 still utilized some unusual hardware. Starting the engine was achieved using a pull-cord, just like the one on your lawn mower. Grab the brake lever, give the cord a few yanks and you were ready to ride. Climb aboard the saddle and rev to 2800 rpm to get things moving.

The engine was fed initially with a Tillotson 38mm carb but testing found that a 36mm Mikuni delivered better results. This 1976 edition features a disc brake at both ends, another industry first. Brakes were an important feature on the RT340 because when you backed off of the throttle there was no engine breaking, just a cycle free-wheeling down the track.

The pair of lay-down rear shocks came from Red-Wing while the front fork was sourced from Betor in Spain. The plastic fenders were products from Preston Petty and did an admirable job of keeping flying dirt off the rider. The front tire was 19 inches in diameter with the rear donut at 18 inches. When compared to some of the other details found on the RT340 the tubular steel frame was almost too typical. The saddle was comfortable for a single rider but a passenger wasn't even given foot pegs, so carrying a friend posed some issues. Three places on the triple tree allowed you install gauges of your choice, but more often the bikes ran with no instruments.

Production of the RT340 ran from 1973 to 1978. Despite some huge wins on the competitive field, declining sales pushed Rokon to the brink of failure. The two-wheel drive Trail-Breakers sold more strongly, but even that wasn't enough to sustain life for Rokon. The business of building the two-wheel drive Rokon was revived in 1981 but it was the only model to continue, the RT was a goner. The fresh example seen here is a rare beast and fully correct. Finding a chassis and powertrain would be tough enough and locating another example as correct as this one would be like asking to live for 200 years. On the day this is being written I found one copy of a complete Rokon RT340 on eBay, but little else in the way of serious bits and pieces. Rokon has gone down in history as a brand many cycle fans have heard of, but will never get a chance to ride or own.

One of the RT340's industry firsts was a disc brake mounted on both ends of the chassis.

Swept high, the exhaust pipe and muffler were also fairly typical for off-road cycles of the day.

Using a Sachs 335cc. single-cylinder, two-stroke engine gave the RT340 a good amount of get-up and go.

One of the more unusual features on the RT340 was the pull start used to get the engine running.

With three different mounting points, hard to see behind the mounting position plate, the RT340 gave the rider suspension options for different tracks and conditions.

Rokon RT340 Model Highlights

The automatic gearbox was the RT340's greatest achievement and it was one of the world's first on a full size motorcycle (Honda offered one in 1976 as well).

The pull-start mechanism was more unusual than helpful, but did get things moving without much effort.

The rear shocks offered three mounting points allowing the rider to customize the response.

A comfortable saddle for one was included but a passenger wasn't given foot pegs.

An 11 inch-diameter disc brake on each wheel provided great stopping power, and it was also an industry first.

The plastic fenders were joined by a plastic fuel tank that held 3 gallons of high octane.

Motorcycle Specifications:
1976 Rokon RT340
Wheelbase: 56.5 inches
Weight: 278 Pounds
Seat Height: 34.5 inches
Displacement: 335cc
Gearbox: CVT (continuously variable automatic)
Final Drive: Chain
Fuel Delivery: 36mm Mikuni
Fuel Capacity: 3 Gallons

Horsepower: 37@6500 RPM
Top Speed: 90 MPH   **MSRP:** $1650
Production: 1973-1976

Motorcycle Ratings
Available Examples: 1 out of 7
Replacement Part Availability: 2 out of 7
Ease of Restoration: 2 out of 7
Final Value vs Restoration Cost:
   1.5 out of 7

1967 Triumph T100C Tiger

Showing off the high-mounted exhaust plated in chrome the Tiger looks ready for action.

Owner: David Freeman

American motorheads have always been in love with cubic inches. Take the case of the Triumph lineup of the 1960s, the spot light always seemed to shine on the larger 650cc bikes, the TR6s and of course, the twin-carb Bonneville. But prospective buyers who walked through any Triumph showroom of the day would find a series of 500cc twins on the floor, some built for the street and some for the dirt, parked right there with their bigger siblings.

In the late 1950s, the then-current 500cc Triumph engine was replaced with a 350cc twin. The new engine offered modern-for-the-time, unit construction, meaning the engine and transmission were contained in the same case. The 650cc bikes wouldn't see a unitized engine and transmission until 1963.

The 350cc engine was soon given an overbore to 69mm. When combined with the stock stroke of 65.5mm, Triumph had themselves a very compact 490cc engine. The over-square design, and relatively light weight, meant this new engine offered great potential as a competition powerplant. That potential was borne out again and again during the decade of the 1960s, and beyond. At Daytona alone, the 500cc Triumphs won the race three times, 1962, '66 and '67. The unit 500cc engine with its

A single instrument - the speedometer - was used on many of Triumph's C models.

The rubber gaitors are used to keep the legs of the forks clean of dirt and debris.

Displacing 490cc the vertical twin engine provided 41 horsepower which was more than adequate to power the T100C ahead smartly.

four-speed transmission won not only at Daytona, but also at a long list of TT, flat track and enduro-style races.

Though the 650 bikes were in theory faster, the AMA Class C rule of the period gave the flatheads (read H-D) a 750cc upper limit while overhead engine (i.e. everything else including Triumph) had to make do with limit of 500cc for maximum displacement.

As seen here in street trim, the T100C with the small tank and full size wheels looks very much like a TR6 or single carb Bonneville painted the wrong color. Though the bike looks very little like a mud spattered enduro champion, the T100C was indeed a very flexible machine. Equipped with the available wide-ratio gear box, aggressive tires and fenders mounted high off the tires, the T100C won literally hundreds of enduros.

There are certain competition features found on this 1967 C model that were absent from the more mundane street bikes of the same year. Things like the sexy twin high pipes that ran along the bike's left side, the folding foot pegs designed to help riders get over and through obstacles on the track, a smaller, 5-3/4 inch, headlight, and a skid plate to protect the engine.

Common to the T100C, as well as the non-C T100 models and the 650 line, are things like the eyebrow tank badge, first used in 1966, two tone paint and that certain Triumph silhouette.

Highlights 1967 Triumph T100C Tiger

The T100C was indeed a true on- and off-road scrambler. In the trim seen on this near-perfect example, the T100C was the perfect bike to take for a summer's evening ride with your girlfriend perched on the back. Yet, in the hands of an experienced racer, and with only relatively minor modifications, the same machine could and did win a long, long list of races on the TT, flat track and enduro circuits.

Because they weren't produced in huge numbers when new, and also due to the shortened life-span of the true race machines, T100Cs are a little harder to find than some of the more common and popular Triumphs from the same period.

Though you might think that parts are harder to find for the 500cc bikes, the truth is that parts availability is just as good for both families of Triumph twins.

Up until recently, the value of the 500cc bikes lagged behind that of similar 650cc models in the same condition - but that has begun to change. Auction prices and on-line prices for bikes like the T100C are coming up fast. If the trend continues they will soon be selling for prices equal to the prices paid for their bigger brothers.

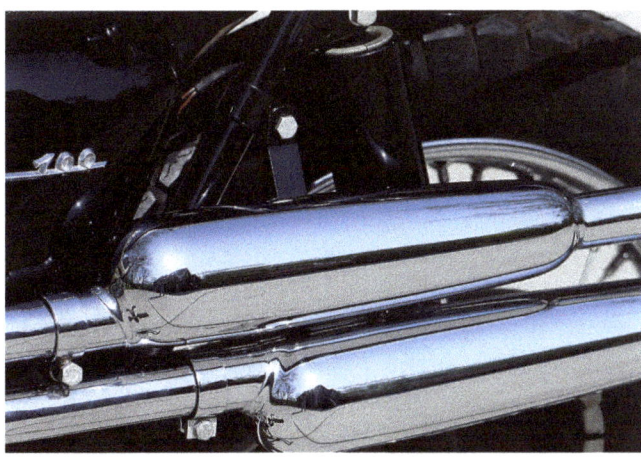

Unlike many of Triumph's road machines, and even the TT bikes, the T100C used an exhaust system that ran two pipes side by side along the left side, with one small muffler used on each pipe.

Part of the enduro nature of the T100C was the reduced size fuel tank and headlight since the model was aimed at the dual-sport crowd.

Motorcycle Specifications
Wheelbase: N/A
Weight: 335 Pounds (dry)
Seat Height: N/A
Displacement: 490cc
Gearbox: 4-Speed
Final Drive: Chain
Fuel Delivery: 26mm Amal Carburetor
Fuel Capacity: 2.5 Gallons
Horsepower: 41@7200 RPM

Top Speed: 100 MPH
MSRP: $1199

Motorcycle Ratings
Available Examples: 3 out of 7
Availability or Replacement Parts: 3 out of 7
Ease of Restoration: 3 out of 7
Final Value vs Restoration Costs: 5 out of 7

1967 Triumph Tiger Cub

Owner: Baxter Cycle

In 1939 Triumph opted to eliminate single-cylinder models from the catalog so they could spend all of their resources on the more popular twin-cylinder variants. Nearly 13 years later the market was once again asking for single-cylinder motorcycles and Triumph answered the call. Previous buyers knew that a Triumph single would still be efficient and easy to ride yet retain the traditional Triumph quality. To respond to this demand the T15 Terrier was released in 1952. A 149cc, single cylinder mill was placed in the frame but the resulting machines were never a big seller.

1954 saw the introduction of the Tiger Cub, fitted with a larger 199cc engine, based on the Terrier engine but with more displacement and 10 more horsepower. The Cub was available in two versions. The T20S was the sportier version meant for road use. The trials version was labeled the T20T. The T20T also had a lower compression engine better suited for trials riding.

Early examples used the plunger-type rear suspension, but for 1957 and beyond, a swingarm with standard shock absorbers was used.

The wheelbase measured only 49 inches and the listed weight was 220 pounds. A four-speed gearbox was included in the mix as were a pair of drum brakes. The reduced power of the trials model was listed as 10@6000 RPM with the sport version claiming 14.5@6500 RPM.

Perhaps the best thing about the Cub was the way it mimicked the look and proportions of the bigger Triumphs of the period. The seat, the fenders, and especially the tank with the Triumph badge and rubber

A nice dual-sport motorcycle, the 1967 Cub was the last of the breed. In 1968 the model was replaced by a BSA-sourced TR25W.

Part of the Cub's visual appeal and popularity came from its resemblance to the bigger Triumphs.

knee pads, looked like they were borrowed directly from the bigger bikes - and helped the Cub look bigger than it really was.

The year 1967 was the last year of production for the Cub. By that time, the take over of Triumph by BSA was taking hold in a big way. The Cub's replacement, the TR25W, came to the dealerships with a BSA-sourced single and very little of the aesthetics that made the Cub look so much like a true Triumph.

1967 Triumph T20T Tiger Cub Highlights

The Tiger Cub was a popular model that was based in its smaller sibling the Terrier.

Light weight and adequate horsepower made the T20T fun to ride and easy to handle on unpaved surfaces.

The Cub used the look and proportions of the bigger Triumphs to great advantage.

The saddle too looked like something borrowed from a T110, though it was only big enough for a rider and passenger if they were really close friends.

The very Triumph looking gas tank held 3.6 gallons and came complete with rubber knee pads.

When the rear suspension was upgraded in 1957 to a swingarm and shocks in the rear the Tiger Cub became a far more competent machine.

The Cub was then, and is now, a very affordable Triumph.

Based on the Terrier's 150cc engine, the 200cc Cub single retained all the strengths of that design: The unitized engine and four-speed transmission, the overhead valves and the modern alternator housed under the left side primary cover.

Motorcycle Specifications:
Wheelbase: 49 inches
Weight: 220 pounds (dry)
Seat Height: N/A
Displacement: 199cc
Gearbox: 4-Speed
Final Drive: Chain
Fuel Delivery: Amal (early '54-'57), Zenith (late '58 and beyond)
Fuel Capacity: 3.6 Gallons
Horsepower: 10@6000 RPM

Top Speed: 66 Miles per Hour
MSRP: N/A

Motorcycle Ratings:
Available Examples: 3 out of 7
Availability of Replacement Parts: 4 out of 7
Ease of Restoration: 5 Out of 7
Final Value vs Restoration Costs: 2 out of 7

1966 Triumph T120 TT

Owner: Keith Campbell

Triumph first opened their doors in 1902, and the marque has enjoyed a long and varied history since then. In 1938 Triumph introduced the 500cc Speed Twin - and from that point to 1983, the success of Triumph was due primarily to the lasting appeal and durability of that one design

The history of the Triumph vertical twin is one of constant improvement and yearly increases in power and torque. The first factory 650cc Triumph, the Thunderbird, was introduced after the war. Spin-offs from the T-bird, like the T110, offered more power from the same 650cc block. The main motivator for the never ending boosts in power came from the US - then as now, American riders always figure a little too much is never quite enough.

By the late 1950s Triumph made the decision to introduce a whole new model - the legendary Bonneville. Equipped with two Amal carbs and hot camshafts, the new hot rod model from Triumph put out nearly 50 horsepower.

Though the numerical model designations used for the Bonneville were a little confusing at first, by 1961 Triumph offered two Bonnevilles, a T120R and T120C - R for Road and C for Competition. The C model Bonnies differed very little from the stock R model bikes. The biggest difference in the first few years of C bikes was the addition of twin high pipes that ran along either side, and the Trials-pattern tires used in place of typical road rubber.

The first true TT bike was offered for sale in 1963. Offered in white without any stripes on the tank, the same color as the stock road-going Bonneville, the

The profile of this 1966 T120 TT Special is true Triumph, stripped to the bare essentials.

Stripped of the luggage rack and wearing the eyebrow tank badge, the slim 2-1/2 gallon tank is the same tank used on street going Bonnevilles. The Alaskan white paint with stripes is likewise identical to the color and design used on the Bonneville tanks.

first TT bike was a true hot rod Triumph that could win races right out of the crate. To ensure the new bike could and would win, the factory installed larger Amal carburetors, hotter cams, and a lot more compression - as in 12 to 1! In the hands of a rider like Eddie Mulder, the TT bikes became an unstoppable weapon against all lesser machines.

The TT bike was first conceived by Johnson Motors, the western US distributor of Triumphs. Desert racing was big in the west, while eastern competition events were often centered on TT tracks. Thus there were eastern and western versions of the true TT bikes, with subtle differences like the finish on the fenders. In 1965 and '66, for example, western bikes came with raw aluminum fenders, while eastern bikes used painted fenders.

The true TT bikes came minus any lighting equipment, painted the same color as that year's Bonneville. What we think of as TT-pipes, weren't actually seen in use until 1965. Bikes built in 1963 and '64 came with the high pipes used on earlier C model Bonnevilles, but with a straight piece of chrome tubing used at the tail end in place of the small mufflers. It's interesting to note that Triumph offered both C model Bonnevilles, and true TT bikes for sale all the way to 1965.

There are a few more things that everybody knows about TT bikes that aren't necessarily true: The first TT bikes did arrive at dealers with the stock parcel grids on the tank, which were often discarded by riders who then filled the tank-holes with small rubber plugs available from the dealer. Because the TT bikes are among the most valuable of the old Triumphs, some Bonnevilles have been restored as TT bikes. And, though the first TT bikes were introduced in 1963, Triumph didn't code the engine numbers with a TT designation until part way through the 1966 model year. Prior to that, the engines for both the C models

The first-year Triumph TT bike with painted fenders and the same high pipes used on earlier C Models, minus the small mufflers.

The TT bikes used 1-3/16 inch amals in place of the 1-1/16 inch carbs used on street Bonnies. The '63 models came with Triumph's ET ignition, and 12 to 1 compression.

1965 was the first year for the true TT pipes. After '63, both the compression and the gearing were lowered.   1963 and '65 bikes from H.C. Morris - photos Timothy Remus.

and the TT bikes were coded T120C. Possible re-stamping of cases is another issue, when they did start to stamp them with a double T, it was done with one stamp, whereas the counterfeiters do it later as an add-on with one T stamp used twice - meaning the stamping just isn't as clean.

You can buy nice TT bikes all day long, either on-line or at a antique bike auction, but you have to use a measure of common sense. The typically high prices mean there's incentive for creative assembly and restoration techniques. Look for a reputable owner/dealer, and good documentation. Sometimes it's worth the extra money to buy from someone with a sterling reputation just to make sure the bike is what it's supposed to be.

No one knows exactly why, but Triumph stopped production of TT bikes after 1967, thus this Aubergine and white example is the last of a very special breed. Bike owned by Baxter Cycle, photo Timothy Remus.

1966 Triumph T120TT model highlights

The visual appeal and race pedigrees of the TT ranks high among collectors, there simply aren't many Triumphs, or vintage motorcycles of any brand, that have the same cool factor as a nice clean TT.

Because of the high value of these bikes, most collectors don't ride them once they've been restored, they become motorcycle art.

TT bikes can be found for sale at auctions and on-line, but the prices are never cheap.

Because they were built in limited numbers, and often abused to death in the desert and on various TT tracks, there just aren't very many true TT bikes out there - which is part of what keeps the value so high.

Motorcycle Specifications:
1966 Triumph T120TT
Wheelbase: 54.5 inches
Weight: 363 Pounds (dry)
Seat Height: 32.5 inches
Displacement: 649cc (two cylinder)
Gearbox: 4-Speed
Final Drive: Chain
Ful Delivery: 1-3/16 in. Amal Monobloc Carburetors
Fuel Capacity: 2.5 Gallons
Horsepower: 47@6500 RPM
Top Speed: N/A
MSRP: $950

Motorcycle Ratings:
Available Examples: 2 out of 7
Availability of Replacement Parts:
  6 out of 7
Ease of Restoration: 5 out of 7
Final Value vs Restoration Costs:
  5 out of 7

1973 Triumph TR5T

Owner: Norm Carroll

As mentioned earlier in this book, BSA bought controlling interest in Triumph way back in early 1951, but the event went unnoticed by nearly everyone in the motorcycle business until the late 1960s when the BSA Group began to take more and more control of what went on at Triumph. It was during the late '60s and early '70s that classic Triumph features and models began to go by the wayside, replaced by designs that originated with BSA.

The Bonneville and TR6s of 1971, with their too-tall, oil-in-frame chassis and missing styling cues, are a good example. The TR5T is another example of BSA-think. Rather than give the T100 line a true makeover, the new regime discovered that Triumph's unit 500cc engine could be squeezed into a BSA frame, meant originally to house a BSA B50 single-cylinder engine.

If true off-road race bikes are supposed to be both light and powerful, the 5T is a complete failure. The 500cc engine, in a mild state of tune, put out something on the order of 30 horses while smaller two-cycle engine of the period made more. Worse, the combined weight of the twin cylinder engine, BSA frame and assorted bits like fenders and a complete gauge set, meant it weighed in at roughly 350 pounds.

The trick is in realizing that this bike was never really meant to be a competition machine. Triumph did, however, enter a group of TR5Ts in the ISDT competition (and they actually made a good showing), but those bikes were far removed from stock models like the one seen here.

Just because the 5T didn't weigh 225 pounds or come to the track with 45 horses

Built after the BSA takeover of Triumph was in full effect, the TR5T is an amalgam of BSA frame and Triumph 500cc twin engine.

Built more for play than off-road competition, The TR5T only enjoyed a two year production run.

For the 1973 model year the front half of the tank was finished in yellow, the 1974 models used the same design with red applied instead of yellow.

The 500cc twin came to the TR5T party with low 9 to 1 compression, a single Amal carb and relatively low gearing - ideal for putting rather than racing.

under the hood, doesn't mean it was a bad bike - if you realize from the get go the things that this bike is good at. Things like riding two up down a gravel road in the country. Or motoring along at 60 miles per hour on a narrow asphalt highway in northern Vermont or Minnesota.

As delivered in the 5T, Triumph's 500cc engine was tuned for torque and easy running, with 9 to 1 compression, and a single Amal carburetor the 5T was the perfect play bike. Geared for torque and not speed, with a somewhat unique exhaust tucked away under the bike and nowhere near your leg or your partner's leg, the bike made a great platform for the right rider.

Despite that modest success, the bike was only in production for two years. No, it wasn't bad sales numbers that spelled the end of the 5T, it was the famous worker's strike at Triumph's Meriden plant that brought down the over-weight and underpowered yet successful play bike. By the time the strike was settled, decisions were made to streamline production - which meant the end of all the 500cc Triumph models.

Highlights of the Triumph TR5T

Maybe not really good at any one thing, the TR5T is instead reasonably good at a lot of things.

This is one vintage triumph that you may want to ride, rather than moth-ball and store in the barn or office.

Despite the short life of the model, TR5Ts are still available. One vintage bike dealer reports that selling one is easy, they never stay for sale for very long.

Like the other 500cc Triumph that precedes this one, interest in the bike is increasing, as are prices. And parts are not so tough to find as you might think.

Motorcycle Specifications:
1973-1974 Triumph TR5T Wheelbase: 54.5 inches
Weight: 350 Pounds (fully fueled)
Seat Height: N/A   Displacement: 490cc
Gearbox: 4-Speed   Final Drive: Chain
Fuel Delivery: 28mm AMAL Concentric Fuel Capacity: 2.4 Gallons
Horsepower: 30@7500 RPM

Top Speed: 75 MPH   MSRP: $1425
Production: 1973-1974

Motorcycle Ratings
Available Examples: 3 out of 7
Replacement Parts Availability: 5 out of 7
Ease of Restoration: 4 out of 7
Final Value vs Restoration Cost: 4 out of 7

1968 Yamaha DT-1

Owner: Brad Powell

The first Yamahas landed on US shores in 1961 and as the years flew by their catalog expanded and the brand grew more popular. By the time 1968 came to be the sport of off-road riding and racing had become a phenomenon in the US with riders of all sizes anxious to get into the fun. There were several choices in the day but many were European brands that were heavy and expensive, both a deterrent to a new rider. The debut of the DT-1 from Yamaha was as significant as the Honda CB750 that followed for 1969.

The DT-1 was not as purpose built as the overseas models and could be ridden to the track, raced and ridden back home again. What it may have lacked in cutting edge technology found on some of the European models it made up for with user friendly hardware, and a price that almost anyone could afford. The 246cc engine delivered 18 horsepower and the DT-1 weighed only 230 pounds prior to adding fuel. The tank held 2.5 gallons allowing the DT-1 to go a nice distance in between stops. The single-cylinder engine was a two-stroke design and typical for the era. It was the overall combination of quality, power and ease of access that propelled the 1968 DT-1 to sales of 50,000 units! In a time when 5000 was considered a great sales number you can see how ten times that would make a huge impact in the market.

Part of that figure was due to the MSRP of only about $520.00. Although not a small fee in 1968 the bike delivered an enormous amount of value for the price, which was less than many of the competing models at the time.

The Yamaha was one of those bikes you kicked to life and it was off to the races, the local gravel pit, or the corner store, all with equal ease.

The success of the 1968 DT-1 set records for sales, the design and construction of the machine made it easy to understand why.

The balance of comfort, power and suspension delivered an unbeatable setup and all at a cost of about $520.

Sold in any color you wanted as long as that was white, the DT-1 offered a comfortable saddle and a neutral ergonomic package for riders of nearly all sizes. A wheelbase of 54.7 inches combined with a seat height of thirty inches and a 230 pound weight made the DT-1 a package nearly any rider could handle.

That overall combination of specs, adequate power and convenience pushed the Yamaha into the sales stratosphere and helped to move the manufacturer into new regions of success. The US dealers had trouble keeping the DT-1 in stock.

With that many bikes sold in a single year you'd think they'd be as common as door knobs today, but that doesn't seem to be the case. A goodly number of compatible parts are available without a lot of searching, but finding a complete motorcycle is another story. Finding one as pristine as that seen here will set you back a number near the top of the range but will be worth every cent as restoring one to this caliber will cost even more.

1968 Yamaha DT-1 Model Highlights

The low retail price helped the DT-1 find its way into nearly 50,000 homes in its first year.

A comfortable saddle and ease of operation were parts of that successful equation.

Adequate suspension travel and 10 inches of ground clearance made the DT-1 a terrific option for a wide variety of riders.

Designed to be a multi-purpose machine the DT-1 could be ridden to the track, raced and ridden back home with ease. It also made a great off-road play bike.

Before adding fuel the DT-1 weighed only 230 pounds which was on par with others on the market.

Eighteen horsepower doesn't sound like much, but coupled to a five-speed transmission and pushing only 230 pounds, it was more than adequate.

A low seat height of 29.8 inches put the smaller riders in line to buy the DT-1, since many other machines were two or more inches taller.

The high-mounted exhaust was complete with expansion chamber and heat shield.

Motorcycle Specifications:
1968 Yamaha DT-1
Wheelbase: 54.7 inches
Weight: 230 Pounds (dry)
Seat Height: 29.8 inches
Displacement: 246cc
Gearbox: 5-Speed   *Final Drive:* Chain
Fuel Delivery: 26mm Mikuni Carburetor
Fuel Capacity: 2.5 Gallons
Horsepower: 18@6000 RPM

Top Speed: 70 MPH (approx.)
MSRP: $520

Motorcycle Ratings
Available Examples: 2 out of 7
Availability of Replacement Parts:
  5 out of 7
Ease of Restoration: 4 out of 7
Final Value vs Restoration Costs:
  4 out of 7

1971 Yamaha RT-1B 360

With the exhaust and heat shield mounted on the right side, the left side view gives a us a cleaner look at the RT-1B's layout.

Owner: Rex Cusumano

Based on the wild success of the DT-1, Yamaha upped the ante for 1970 and introduced the RT-1. Powered by a bigger 351cc motor, it promised to be a big hit. Riders who spent time on and off-road could use the talents of the newest model in the Yamaha family seven days a week.

1971 was the second year of production for the RT-1 and was hence called the RT-1B in typical Yamaha tradition. Tipping the scales at 268 pounds with a half a tank of fuel, the RT-1B made short work of nearly any trail. Ten inches of ground clearance assured the rider he'd return home without bashing the bottom of his motor on an obstacle, a skid plate assisted in that attempt. The single-cylinder, two-stroke motor produced 30 horsepower at 6000 RPM, magazine reviews of the day said it pulled from 2500 RPM all the way to 6500 without stopping to catch its breath. A five-speed gearbox offered enough ratios to tackle changing terrain, or a trip to the local Dairy Queen. The RT-1 came with a full set of gauges, the speedo and tachometer mounted just above the headlight.

The Mikuni VM 32mm carburetor delivered a precise amount of fuel regardless of the demands being placed on the machine. Two and a half gallons of dead dinosaurs could be squeezed into the narrow tank

Attached to the side of the muffler we find a chrome-plated heat shield meant to protect the rider's leg from burns.

Intended for use both on- and off-road, the RT-1B was equipped with both speedometer and tachometer.

The combination of light weight, a relatively large 351cc engine and 5 speed transmission made the RT-1 a strong running motorcycle.

designed to give the rider plenty of leg room when the trail got narrow. A head and tail light were joined by turn signals, making the RT-1B legal to ride on the streets, even after sundown. Period reviews weren't enamored with the front turn signals as they looked like afterthoughts hung from the handlebars. Designed primarily for solo riding there were no passenger pegs offered on the RT-1.

The blacked-out exhaust swept high on the chassis was equipped with a chrome heat shield to prevent the rider's legs from getting toasted. The chassis is similar in design to the DT-1 but was reinforced to cope with the added weight and power of the bigger engine. Even with the added weight and increased power the RT-1B achieved good mileage ratings of 49 MPG, making it an easy choice for those who used their Yamaha for daily transportation.

A chrome front fender hugged the tire closely and was fairly easy to damage when on the open trails. Drum brakes at both ends helped to slow the RT-1B down with confidence, in as much as drum brakes could. Even with ten inches of ground clearance the saddle was fairly close to the ground at 31.5 inches and the Yamaha square-section handlebar brace was on hand for added rigidity.

Popularity of the RT-1B when new carries over in today's market and you can find a nice variety of machines and the parts required to bring them back to life. Once returned to the fold you'll get years of pleasure out of your RT-1B, just like buyers did in 1970 and '71. When new they asked $925 at your local dealer and I suspect finding one in great condition now will set you back more than that.

Yamaha DT-1B Model Highlights

A terrific power band with great frame and handling made this one of Yamaha's best.

A relatively low saddle height combined

Given the year of manufacture, it's not surprising to find a drum brake at the rear, and also at the front of the RT-1.

Once it exits the engine the exhaust moves high and tucks in close to the frame.

with plenty of ground clearance meant the DT-1B could tackle almost any type of terrain.

The modest MSRP didn't keep buyers away, especially when realizing how much they got for the asking price.

Low weight and better than average fuel economy meant you could happily use the DT-1B to hit the track or ride to work.

When it came to ergonomics, the reinforced handlebars and comfortable seat definitely delivered.

Equipped with a lot more engine than its predecessor the DT-1, the RT-1B was still not a hard bike to start.

The black paint and chrome fenders made for a good looking motorcycle.

Motorcycle Specifications:
1971 Yamaha DT-1B 360
Wheelbase: 54.7 inches
Weight: 268 Pounds (1/2 tank of fuel)
Seat Height: 31.5 inches
Displacement: 351cc
Gearbox: five-speed
Final Drive: Chain
Fuel Delivery: Mikuni VM 32mm SH Carburetor
Fuel Capacity: 2.5 Gallons
Horsepower: 30@6000 RPM

Top Speed: 84 MPH
MSRP: $925
Production: 1970 -1971

Motorcycle Ratings
Available Examples: 3 out of 7
Replacement Parts Availability:
  4 out of 7
Ease of Restoration: 4 out of 7
Final Value vs Restoration:
  Cost: 3 out of 7

1967 Yamaha YM2C Big Bear Scrambler

You can view either side of the YM2C and witness nearly identical views of this classic Yamaha.

Owner: Roger Smith

Yamaha arrived in the states only three years after Honda and for the first few years had only tiny, pressed-steel-frame cycles in their catalog. As people became aware of the brand and the charming, friendly cycles being offered, the company continued to grow. Two-stroke engines were all the company had to offer, no one from Japan would change that until many years later. The number of models, displacements and features continued to expand along with Yamaha's sales numbers.

For 1967 Yamaha introduced a new model for the North American market only. The YM2C, also known as the Big Bear Scrambler, combined many features of other machines and was Yamaha's first "scrambler" entry. The name suggested that the new Yamaha was capable of both on, and off-road fun. As designed, about the only things making the scramblers capable of off-road activity was the high-mounted exhaust and the crossbar on the handlebars. The tires themselves were nothing more than street level items, lacking any sort of extra tread as found on the knobby tires mounted on true dirt bikes.

Although lacking what was needed to hit a rugged trail, the Big Bear Scrambler still presented an appealing raft of features that made it a great draw to buyers in the USA.

Named for the famous Big Bear race in California the YM2C was far from capable of performing in that event, but it looked great and buyers flooded the showrooms to get one of their own. A pair of 24mm Mikuni carbs fed the 305cc twin-cylinder engine, while a matched set of chrome exhaust pipes sent the spent fumes packing. The slotted heat shields were also finished in chrome, as was the fuel tank and fenders.

The factory specs claimed the Big Bear Scrambler could climb a 23 degree slope and I suppose if conditions weren't too rough that would be doable. The close-fitting fenders would allow loose dirt and debris to fill the space quickly, wreaking havoc on traction and control.

Yamaha's own "Autolube" system kept the two-stroke mill lubed up without concern from the rider - eliminating the need to mix gas and oil. When filled with fuel the YM2C weighed 360 pounds which was fairly substantial in the off-road universe but no hindrance on the street. Horsepower was rated at 30@7000 RPM, top speed was rated at 80 MPH.

The Big Bear's MSRP of only $700 was just one of the many reasons for the bike's wild popularity, in fact more than 6000 were sold in its only year of sale. The fact that they were so popular when new and built in high numbers means finding one today isn't a real struggle. Finding one complete with its original exhaust is another story all together, but there seems to be multiple sources for parts online. Riding a Big Bear Scrambler when they were new was entertaining, and riding one today is sure to put a smile on your face.

Year-to-Year Changes

Sadly the popular Big Bear Scrambler was only sold for one year in the USA and was quickly supplanted by Yamahas with bigger engines and more features, making the YM2C an instant classic and highly desired among collectors today.

Fed by a pair of 24mm Mikuni carbs, the compact engine displaced a healthy 305cc and made 30 horsepower.

The chrome plated, slotted-steel heat shields used on both sides of the Big Bear looked great but may not have provided too much protection from burns.

Plated in chrome and accented by the color of your choice, plus the rubber knee pads, gave the YM2C a classic look that sill endures.

The side cover on the right side of the Big Bear touted Yamaha's Autolube system which eliminated the need to mix gas and oil.

A 51 inch wheelbase gave the Big Bear Scrambler a compact look but provided plenty of stability whether riding on the street or trails.

1967 Yamaha YM2C Model Highlights

Wearing a high amount of chrome really added to the appeal of the Big Bear Scrambler when it was new and still draws your eye today.

The powerful twin-cylinder 305cc engine produced 30 ponies and propelled the YM2C along smartly.

An MSRP of only $700 did nothing to turn buyers away, and more than 6000 bikes were sold in the only year of sale.

A comfortable saddle that could accommodate two helped make the bike very user friendly.

A four gallon fuel tank permitted more miles between refills but was a bit of a drawback when riding in off-road mode.

You could get your Big Bear Scrambler in blue, red or black, which meant yours wouldn't necessarily look exactly like every other Big Bear on the road.

The chrome fuel tank was another great visual feature that added to the overall mix of great features found on the YM2C.

The all-in-one gauge provided the rider with a speedometer, tachometer and several warning lights in one housing.

Motorcycle Specifications:
1967 Yamaha YM2C Big Bear Scrambler
Wheelbase: 51 inches
Weight: 360 Pounds (full tank of fuel)
Seat Height: N/A
Displacement: 305cc
Gearbox: 5-Speed
Final Drive: Chain
Fuel Delivery: (2) 24mm Mikuni Carburetors
Fuel Capacity: 4 Gallons
Horsepower: 30@7000 RPM

Top Speed: 80 MPH   *MSRP:* $700
Production: 1967 and only sold in North America

Motorcycle Ratings:
Available Examples: 3 out of 7
Replacement Parts Availability:
  4 out of 7
Ease of Restoration: 4 out of 7
Final Value vs Restoration Cost:
  4 out of 7

1974 Yankee 500Z

Other than the two-cylinder engine, the rest of the Yankee was pretty typical, except perhaps for the rear disc brake - a first for motorcycles of the period.

Owner: Rex Cusumano

John Taylor was in the business of importing OSSA motorcycles in the late '60s but dreamt of a more powerful machine that could be used on and off-road. There were many 500cc machines already populating the off-road world but each one was powered by a single cylinder engine. Commonly referred to "thumpers" due to their pounding single cylinder.

John designed a two-cylinder engine with cylinders that would fire at the same time, unlike a more typical two-cylinder with cylinders that were always on opposite cycles - i.e. when one cylinder was on the power stroke the other was on the intake stroke. Keeping the cylinders on opposite cycles helped to reduce vibration for street use. For dirty work, however, a little extra vibration isn't necessarily a bad thing.

By firing the cylinders at th the same time, John produced a 500cc twin with the dirt-friendly torque characteristics of a single.

The 500Z was a stout machine that bristled with an array of unique features. The chrome-moly frame delivered light weight and plenty of rigidity. A rear disc brake was the first of its kind and the low gear on the six-speed gearbox could be locked out to comply with AMA rules of the period. Stainless steel handlebars were also a first

A muffler was found on each side of the chrome-moly frame, but they didn't do much to tame the noise coming from the engine.

The front fender was adorned with the same style of striping found on the fuel tank.

The Yankee's own twin-cylinder engine displaced 488cc. Fed by a pair of 24mm IRZ carburetors the twin produce 40 horsepower at 6500 RPM.

as was the flat-sided oval swingarm. The configuration provided added stiffness without any added weight. With a half-tank of fuel the 500Z still weighed-in at 349 pounds, hardly a lightweight machine. The added heft wasn't much of a problem when the 500Z was ridden on the street, but hampered severe off-road efforts. A top speed of just over 85 miles per hour was possible making the 500Z one of the faster dual-purpose machines of the day.

The wheelbase of 53.5 inches was shorter than many including Honda's 250 Motosport which carried 2-1/2 more inches between its wheels.

Silver paint with yellow accent stripes was applied to all the sheet metal, on every copy of the 500Z. The small head and tail lights allowed the 500Z to be legally ridden on the street.

When John began designing the 500Z the market was only beginning to see new models roll in. Once production began he was faced with a wealth of competing machines, nearly all of which delivered better performance on an off-road course. Carrying a retail price of $1495 did not help the Yankee, as many similar bikes from other manufacturers could be purchased for considerably less.

Total production for the 500Z totaled only 750 units before the Yankee Motorcycle Company closed its doors. As a result of the low production figures, finding one to ride or restore today will be a daunting effort.

1974 Yankee 500Z Model Highlights

The twin-cylinder "thumper" motor was the most unusual feature and delivered terrific power but at an increased decibel level.

Stainless steel handlebars provided a sturdy place for the rider to hold on even in the roughest of conditions.

The ability to lock-out the low gear to meet with the AMA rules also helped the 500Z compete in more classes of off-road events.

The only gauge present was the speedometer-odometer combination.

The 3.25 gallon fuel tank was trimmed with only a basic company name and a set of yellow accent stripes.

Forged aluminum fork crowns were machined by Smith and Wesson the well known firearms maker.

Company graphics on the 500Z were minimal with the large "Z" on the side covers being the most obvious.

Capable of traveling at 85 miles per hour permitted the 5000Z to be taken on nearly any road, paved or not, for extra saddle time.

The profile of the Yankee wasn't as radical as many of its features. In today's world it would take a minor miracle to locate a Yankee this nice.

Motorcycle Specifications:
1974 Yankee 500Z
Wheelbase: 53.5 inches
Weight (half tank of fuel) 349 Pounds
Seat Height: 33 inches
Displacement: 488cc
Gearbox: Six-Speed
Final Drive: Chain
Fuel Delivery: (2) IRZ 24mm
Fuel Capacity: 3.25 Gallons
Horsepower: 40@6500

Top Speed: 85 Miles Per Hour
MSRP: $1495
Production: 1973-1974 (750)

Motorcycle Ratings:
Available Example: 1 out of 7
Replacement Parts Availability:
** 1 out of 7**
Ease of Restoration: 1 out of 7
Final Value vs Restoration Cost:
** 1 out of 7**

1967 Zundapp 100 ISDT

The small size did nothing to dispel the worthiness of the 100 ISDT as it took on all comers in its factory race trim, this model being a replica sold through American Eagle dealers in the USA.

Owner: John Young

The German Zundapp brand came to be in 1917. Their first creations carried 211cc and 246cc powerplants and as the company progressed so did their ambitions. Continued expansion of the motorcycle market allowed the company to deliver a variety of motorcycles to fit with the needs of a variety of riders. The growing interest level of riders in the off-road bikes that occurred in the 1960s didn't go unnoticed by this small firm, and several different models were created to compete against its much larger rivals.

The 100 ISDT was crafted to compete in the grueling international six-day trials events held around the world. Each event required every cycle to be sealed and wired to avoid changes and repairs from being made as the riders spent six days traversing all sorts of rough terrain and obstacles. A machine for these races needed to be nimble, powerful and reliable, features which were very challenging in the late '60s.

This model from Zundapp was a replica of the factory entry that won the ISDT two years in a row. At the Greenhorn Enduro it "whipped all entries including some 360 Husqvarna and 650 Triumphs," according to the sales brochure. Sold through the

American Eagle franchise, the tiny machine also earned high credits from CYCLE magazine, claiming "Zundapp is all motorcycle, smooth and strong."

Built around a heavy gauge center tube frame, the 100 ISDT weighed only 186 pounds dry and sported 9.3 horsepower at 7200 RPM. The 100cc two-stroke engine included a 4-speed gearbox in the same case, and rolled on a 49 inch wheelbase. The high-mounted exhaust was chrome plated and took an odd path from the engine to the fender when viewed from above. The perforated heat shield was a part of the plan and did as much as any of them could in preventing burns to the rider's leg.

Released as an enduro version of the actual race bike means the 100 ISDT was fitted with head and tail lights as well as a tire-hugging front fender with semi-knobby tires at each end. A basic speedometer was installed into the top of the headlight bezel and the fuel tank held a generous 3.3 gallons of fuel to extend your riding time, beyond what was offered by most other 100cc machines.

All in all the diminutive Zundapp provided the buyer with a confident machine despite its reduced dimensions. Hydraulic forks up front and coil-over springs in the rear provided plenty of comfort and the well-padded saddle only added to the ease of operation on the street or trails.

This is another machine that was never built in huge numbers, making locating a nice example a challenge. The same holds true for any required restoration bits and pieces. Taking on the challenge will prove to be daunting but the end result will be a machine that still performs well even after 4 decades of newer technology have come into view.

Displacing 100cc and delivering just over 9 horsepower the ISDT was not going to win any drag races.

The two-tone finish looks great and the tank can hold 3.3 gallons of fuel.

The conical exhaust tapered and bent to follow the lines of the chassis and was fitted with a perforated heat shield plated in chrome.

Zundapp 100 ISDT Model Highlights

Weighing only 186 pounds before adding fuel, the 100 ISDT replica made for a nimble machine with great capabilities.

Ten inches of ground clearance allowed the rider to take on some aggressive terrain despite the tiny scale of the cycle.

A 3.3 gallon fuel tank gave the 100 ISDT a nice range that let you enjoy the comfortable saddle for longer than many other machines.

Head and tail lights, with the included speedometer, meant ISDT could be licensed for street use.

The combination of the bright red paint and silver offsets made for an attractive machine.

The 100cc engine stared easily and a 4-speed gearbox was pretty standard for the period.

Deemed an enduro machine, the built-in speedometer was a nice feature.

The Zundapp 100 ISDT was built on a small scale but did well against much bigger machines when the competition got rough.

Motorcycle Specifications:
1967 Zundapp 100 ISDT
Wheelbase: 49 inches
Weight: 186 Pounds (dry)
Seat Height: 32 inches
Displacement: 100cc
Gearbox: 4-Speed
Final Drive: Chain
Fuel Delivery: Carburetor
Fuel Capacity: 3.3 Gallons

Horsepower: 9.3@7200 RPM
Top Speed: N/A   **MSRP:** N/A

Motorcycle Ratings
Available Examples: 2 out of 7
Availability of Replacement Parts:
  2 out of 7
Ease of Restoration: 2 out of 7
Final Value vs Restoration Costs:
  2 out of 7

1973 Zudapp GS125

Left side view of one very compact and business-like Zundapp. Other than the lights and speedo required for enduro events, there isn't anything on the bike that isn't essential to its operation.

Owner: John Young

Still in the throes of the wildly expanding off-road craze, Zundapp released another machine to be included in official races as well as ridden home by enthusiasts.

Slightly bigger than their previous 100 ISDT model, the new model came in two forms: the GS 125 for enduro work and a stripped MC 125 for moto-cross.

Both models were powered by what was essentially the same single-cylinder engine with a displacement of 123.6cc. The rated power on the MC was 19@7900 RPM and the GS was shown having 18@7600. The GS was fitted with a 26mm Bing carb and was rated with a top speed of 66 MPH. Before you fill the tank with 2.64 gallons of fuel the GS weighed only 233 pounds. The exhaust pipe was complete with a small chrome heat shield that was mounted to the matte black pipe and muffler.

Add-ons for the GS included the head and tail lights, a simple speedometer, electric horn and a tool kit. The saddle was listed as a "solo bench" and was well padded for the rider with no accommodations for a passenger. The frame was finished in bright red paint while the fuel tank got a

The black exhaust includes the small wire cage whose job is to protect the rider from burns.

Deemed the enduro model this GS125 came complete with the circular speedo found atop the handlebars.

With a capacity of nearly 3 gallons the fuel tank on the GS125 gave the ride a decent range between fill-ups.

chrome plated finish. Zundapp touted their frame as "non-distorting," the double-loop cradle was manufactured using precision seamless steel tubing. They also claimed that both of their 125s were built to withstand the rigors of trials and MX racing. The claims were backed up by the numerous trophies taken home by Zundapp riders during their long history.

Official sales numbers for the Zundapp are not listed but it's safe to assume that production volume wasn't too high for the GS125. The example pictured here has never been started and is as original as it can be. Finding one in completely original form would be daunting enough but seeking one with no miles would be akin to winning the lottery, twice. There seem to be a fair number of parts listed on eBay but not enough to restore a basket case. As with any restoration project any advance shopping you can do will save you grief down the road.

1973 Zundapp GS125 Model Highlights

The GS 125 is another light weight machine that is aimed at the all-around rider who may spend time on and off-road.

A small yet potent engine propels the compact machine to a claimed top speed of 71.5 MPH.

With a fuel capacity of more than two gallons your range will exceed many others who can barely take more than 1.5 gallons on a journey.

Before adding fuel the GS125 weighs a mere 240 pounds, making it easy to move around and ride on uneven terrain.

The lights, speedo and tool kit on the enduro version make it a convenient machine to ride on or off road.

The radial cylinder head fins - known as a feature on Sachs engines - are used on this Zundapp single for the same reason, to keep the cylinder head nice and cool.

Designed for serious racing, the GS125 is actually the milder version of the two 125 models offered by Zundapp in 1973

Motorcycle Specifications:
1973 Zundapp GS125
Wheelbase: N/A
Weight: 240.3 Pounds (dry)
Seat Height: N/A
Displacement: 123cc
Gearbox: 5-Speed
Final Drive: Chain
Fuel Delivery: 26mm Bing Carburetor
Fuel Capacity: 2.64 Gallons
Horsepower: 18@7600 RPM

Top Speed: 71.5 MPH
MSRP: N/A

Motorcycle Ratings
Available Examples: 2 out of 7
Availability of Replacement Parts: 3 out of 7
Ease of Restoration: 3 out of 7
Final Value vs Restoration Costs: 3 out of 7

Wolfgang Books On The Web

http://www.wolfpub.com

HOW TO BUILD A CAFÉ RACER

What's old is new again, and the newest trend on the block is Café Racers.

Written by well-known motorcycle and automotive author Doug Mitchel, this book starts with the history lesson. And though those first bikes were build in the UK for racing from café to café, the current rage for Café Racers has definitely spread to the US.

Converting a stock motorcycle to a Café Racer requires more than a fairing and a few decals. Doug starts the book with a chapter on planning. Choosing an appropriate bike comes next, followed by chapters that detail the modifications that will likely be embraced by anyone converting a stocker to a rocker. From shocks and tires to engine modifications, Doug's book lays out each type of modification, and how it's best carried through.

Ten Chapters   144 Pages $27.95   Over 400 color images - 100% color

HONDA ENTHUSIASTS GUIDE

Enthusiasts Guide - Honda Motorcycles 1959 to 1985 is designed to aid the non-professional motorcycle collector decide whether or not to buy and restore Honda motorcycles produced between 1959 and 1985.

For each of these models, author Doug Mitchel provides four to six paragraphs describing the bike in general terms including difference and similarities between the model being discussed and other, similar, models.

In addition, bullet point for each model will include the following information: Cost to acquire the project. Value when finished. Which bikes/models should not be restored due to declining value. Where to find the frame and engine numbers. This new book will also include what to look for when checking the condition of items like the paint and decals, chrome, seat, rubber parts, and suspension.

144 Pages $27.95   Over 400 photos - 100% color

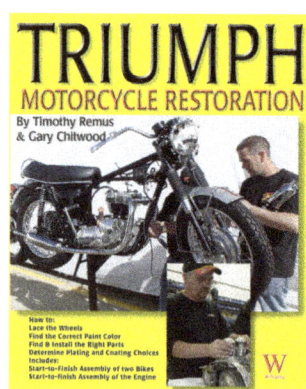

TRIUMPH MOTORCYCLE RESTORATION

Wolfgang Publications offers complete start-to-finish assembly and restoration sequences on two Triumph Twins, a 1963 Bonneville and a 1969 Bonneville. Also included is the start-to-finish assembly of the 1969 engine and transmission. Rather than try to describe the miniscule differences that often separated one year from another, this book offers a color gallery with left and right side views of all significant models from 1959 to 1970. With over 450 color photos, Triumph Restoration offers 144 pages of hard-core how-to help for anyone who wants to repair or restore their own Triumph twin.

Seven Chapters   144 Pages $29.95   Over 400 photos - 100% color

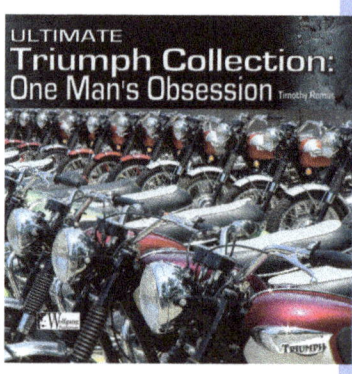

ULTIMATE TRIUMPH COLLECTION

Ultimate Triumph Collection presents 80 perfect Triumphs, from early singles to a perfect Speed Twin, all belonging to one man.

Chapter one describes the builder, Bobby Sullivan, the man with the vision and drive to continue building bikes long after his initial goals were met. Chapter two introduces the team that builds the bikes, and the process of finding individual machines. Chapter three documents nearly 80 pages with studio images of the left and right side of each machine. Chapter four offers photos and anecdotes on the exceptional examples.

Illustrated with abundant images by well-known photographer Timothy Remus, and printed on high quality seventy-pound paper, this ten-by-ten hardcover book is one that any motorcycle enthusiast will want to add to his or her collection.

Four Chapters   144 Pages $59.95 (includes S&H in US)   100% color

For a current list, visit our website
www.wolfpub.com

CUSTOM MOTORCYCLE FABRICATION

Owner of Bare Knuckle Choppers and long time motorcycle builder and fabricator, Paul Wideman is the perfect author for this book. With experience as both a hands-on builder and technical editor for Cycle Source Magazine, Paul has exactly the skill-set needed to write a book on fabrication.

Some commonly fabricated parts like handle bars and exhaust systems are covered as separate topics, along with sections on building simple brackets and mounts.

Learn how professionals like Paul bypass the catalog and build their parts from scratch instead. This is an essential building book, helping you build the necessary skills needed to assemble a truly unique kick-ass motorcycle.

Eleven Chapters   144 Pages $27.95   Over 400 color images - 100% color

LEARNING THE ENGLISH WHEEL

Despite the fact that thousands of English wheel machines have been sold the past ten years there is currently no book dedicated to English wheeling. Owners of these machines are at a loss on how to really use them - because of the lack of DETAILED published material.

This book covers all aspects of English wheeling, from making your own wheel to learning the basics, from fabricating high-crown panels to reverse flares.

The photos used through the book serve to illustrate both what makes up a good English wheel, and how – exactly – to use an English wheel. Side bars and interviews done with famous wheelers and fabricators from around the world help to give personal insight from the best of the best.

Twelve Chapters   144 Pages $27.95   Over 300 photos, 100% color

SHEET METAL BIBLE

Sheet Metal Bible is a compendium of sheet metal fabrication projects, everything from simple shaping operations to multi-piece creations like fenders and motorcycle gas tanks. Each of these operations is photographed in detail. Meaty captions help the reader to understand what's really happening as a flat sheet of steel slowly morphs into the convex side of a gas tank.

While some of the craftsmen work with hand tools, others prefer the English Wheel. The book is filled with work by legendary fabricators like Ron Covell, Craig Naff, Rob Roehl and Bruce Terry.

So whether your project needs parts made from aluminum or steel, is simple or complex, there is something in this new 176 page book to help you turn that dream into reality.

Eight Chapters   176 Pages $29.95   Over 400 photos, 100% color

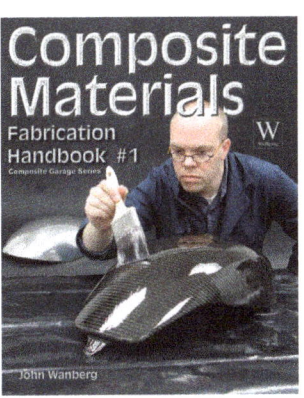

COMPOSITE MATERIALS FABRICATION HANDBOOK #1

While most books on composites approach the subject from a very technical standpoint, Beginning Composites presents practical, hands-on information about these versatile materials. From explanations of what a composite is, to demonstrations on how to actually utilize them in various projects, this book provides a simple, concise perspective on molding and finishing techniques to empower even the most apprehensive beginner.

Topics include: What is a composite, why use composites, general composite types and where composites are typically used. Composite Materials Fabrication Handbook includes shop set up, design and a number of hands-on start-to-finish projects documented with abundant photographs.

Eight Chapters   144 Pages $27.95   Over 300 photos, 100% color

Wolfgang Publication Titles
For a current list visit our website at www.wolfpub.com

ILLUSTRATED HISTORY
Ultimate Triumph Collection	$59.95
American Police Motorcycles - Revised	$24.95

BIKER BASICS
Custom Motorcycle Fabrication	$27.95
Custom Bike Building Basics	$24.95
Sportster/Buell Engine Hop-Up Guide	$24.95
Sheet Metal Fabrication Basics	$24.95
How to Fix American T-Twin Motorcycles	$27.95

COMPOSITE GARAGE
Composite Materials Handbook #1	$27.95
Composite Materials Handbook #2	$27.95
Composite Materials Handbook #3	$27.95

HOT ROD BASICS
How to A/C Your Hot Rod	$24.95
So-Cal Speed Shop's How to Build Hot Rod Chassis	$24.95
Hot Rod Wiring	$27.95
How to Chop Tops	$24.95

CUSTOM BUILDER SERIES
How to Build A Café Racer	$27.95
Advanced Custom Motorcycle Wiring - Revised	$27.95
How to Build an Old Skool Bobber Sec Ed	$27.95
How To Build The Ultimate V-Twin Motorcycle	$24.95
Advanced Custom Motorcycle Assembly & Fabrication	$27.95
How to Build a Cheap Chopper	$27.95

LIFESTYLE
Bean're — Motorcycle Nomad	$18.95
George The Painter	$18.95
The Colorful World of Tattoo Models	$34.95

MOTORCYCLE RESTORATION SERIES
Triumph Restoration - Unit 650cc	$29.95
Triumph MC Restoration Pre-Unit	$29.95

SHEET METAL
Sheet Metal Fab for Car Builders	$27.95
Advanced Sheet Metal Fabrication	$27.95
Ultimate Sheet Metal Fabrication	$24.95
Sheet Metal Bible	$29.95

AIR SKOOL SKILLS
How To Draw Monsters	$27.95
Airbrush Bible	$29.95
How Airbrushes Work	$24.95

PAINT EXPERT
How To Airbrush, Pinstripe & Goldleaf	$27.95
Kosmoski's New Kustom Painting Secrets	$27.95
Pro Pinstripe Techniques	$27.95
Advanced Pinstripe Art	$27.95

TATTOO U Series
Advanced Tattoo Art - Revised	$27.95
Cultura Tattoo Sketchbook	$32.95
Tattoo Sketchbook by Jim Watson	$32.95
Tattoo Sketchbook by Nate Powers	$27.95
Into The Skin The Ultimate Tattoo Sourcebook (Includes companion DVD)	$34.95
American Tattoos	$27.95
Tattoo Bible Book One	$27.95
Tattoo Bible Book Two	$27.95
Tattoo Bible Book Three	$27.95
Tattoo Lettering Bible	$27.95

TRADE SCHOOL SERIES
Learning The English Wheel	$27.95

GUIDE BOOKS
Honda Motorcycles - Enthusiast Guide	$27.95

www.ingramcontent.com/pod-product-compliance
Lightning Source LLC
Chambersburg PA
CBHW041241240426
43668CB00025B/2460